Greater Things To Come

Future Revealed

C. Wilson Hart

authorHOUSE

AuthorHouse™
1663 Liberty Drive
Bloomington, IN 47403
www.authorhouse.com
Phone: 1-800-839-8640

© 2010 C. Wilson Hart. All rights reserved.

No part of this book may be reproduced, stored in a retrieval system, or transmitted by any means without the written permission of the author.

First published by AuthorHouse 2/25/2010

ISBN: 978-1-4490-7905-5 (e)
ISBN: 978-1-4490-7904-8 (sc)
ISBN: 978-1-4490-7903-1 (hc)

Library of Congress Control Number: 2010901347

Printed in the United States of America
Bloomington, Indiana

This book is printed on acid-free paper.

Unless otherwise noted, scriptures are from New International Version of the Bible Copyright 1973, 1978 by the International Bible Society Used by permission of Zondervan Publishing

C. Wilson and his wife Maria are co founders of 'Jesus Cares Ministry' in Canada and the Philippines. This ministry supports abandoned boys and girls taken from the streets of Manila as well as abandoned Seniors. It also supports a Mission School which prepares needy children for a life time of learning. Also providing food, clothing, school supplies and hot meals.
For more information write: Jesus Cares Ministry
        PO. Box 156 - 1750 E 41st Ave.,
        Vancouver, B.C., Canada
        V5P 4N5

        Email: jesuscares@live.ca

TABLE OF CONTENTS

1. INTRODUCTION 1
   A. COMING EVENTS PROPHESIED 1
   B. FUTURE EVENTS REVEALED 3

2. PROPHECIES FOR OUR TIME PROPHECIES OF CHRIST'S LIFE ON EARTH AND HIS RETURN ACCORDING TO THE OLD TESTAMENT 5
   A. PROPHESY REGARDING CHRIST'S FIRST COMING TO EARTH 5
   B. JESUS COMING AS KING 7

3. THE APPEARING OF JESUS CHRIST FOR HIS CHURCH 9
   'A' THE NATURE OF HIS APPEARING 9
   B. THE SIGNS OF HIS APPEARING 11
   C. MANKIND'S ATTITUDE JUST BEFORE CHRIST'S RETURN 12
   D. THE APPEARING OF CHRIST 13
   E. THE RAPTURE OF THE CHURCH 14

4. THE WORLD IN CHAOS 17
   A. THE INVADING ARMIES FORM 17
   B. SATAN IS THROWN TO EARTH 18
   C. THE JEWS ARE WARNED PROTECTED BY GOD 21
   D. ARMIES GO AGAINST THE JEWS 22
   E. GOD PROTECTS HIS CHOSEN ONES 23
   F. THE BEAST APPEARS 25

5. BEFORE TRIBULATION 26
   A. A PEACE TREATY FOR SEVEN YEARS 26
   B. JEWISH TEMPLE IS REBUILT IN JERUSALEM 26
   C. 144,000 SERVANTS OF GOD ISRAELI EVANGELISTS 27
   D. GOD'S ANGEL PROCLAIMS THE GOSPEL 28
   E. THE SEVEN SEALED SCROLL 29

    F. WHY 7 YEARS OF TRIBULATION 30

6. FIRST HALF of TRIBULATION BEGINS WHICH
   LASTS FOR THREE AND A HALF YEARS 34
       A. THE BEAST COMES TO POWER 34
       B. DECEPTION OF THE BEAST 35
       C. POWER TO CONQUER CHRISTIANS 35
       D. THE FALSE PROPHET COMES 36
       E. MARK OF THE BEAST 37
       F. GOD SENDS AN ANGEL- WARNING 37
       G. THE FIRST SEAL IS OPENED BY JESUS 38
       H. DANIEL'S VISION OF THE BEAST 40
       I. ONE WORLD GOVERNMENT 41
       J. APOSTATE RELIGIOUS ORDER 42
       K. MARTYRED SAINTS 45
       L. BEAST DESTROYS RELIGIOUS ORDER 47
       M. EARTH REDEEMED BY GOD 48
       N. FIRST HALF OF TRIBULATION ENDS 49

7. MID TRIBULATION BEGINS 50
       A. 144,000 TAKEN TO HEAVEN 50
       B. SECOND HARVEST OF BELIEVERS 51
       C. END OF SACRIFICES IN THE TEMPLE 52
       D. ORDER BREAKS DOWN 53
       E. SECOND SEAL IS OPENED - PEACE ENDS 54
       F. GOD'S PRESENCE ARE TWO WITNESSES 55

8. JUDGEMENTS BEGIN 56
       A. SEVEN TRUMPET JUDGEMENTS 56
       B. THE THIRD SEAL IS OPENED 61
       C. THE FOURTH SEAL IS OPENED 62
       D. SEVEN BOWL JUDGEMENTS 64
       E. THE FIFTH SEAL IS OPENED 65
       F. THE SIXTH SEAL IS OPENED 69

9. JESUS TAKES BACK TITLE DEED TO THE EARTH 71
       A. JESUS TAKES BACK THE EARTH 71
       B. JESUS REVEALS HIS OWN 71

    C. THE TWO WITNESSES   72
    D. CELEBRATION IN HEAVEN   73

10. ARMIES ARRIVE IN ISRAEL   75
    A. PREPARATION FOR ARMAGEDDON   75
    B. THE SEVENTH SEAL IS OPENED   76

11. JESUS RETURNS TO THE EARTH   78
    A. RETURN OF JESUS AND HIS SAINTS   78
    B. WEDDING SUPPER OF THE LAMB   78
    C. BATTLE OF ARMAGEDDON   80
    D. THE THIRD HARVEST   81
    E. BEAST AND FALSE PROPHET INTO LAKE OF
       FIRE   83
    F. SATAN INTO THE ABYSS   83
    G. JUDGES GIVEN AUTHORITY   84

12. THE MILLENNIAL KINGDOM AND REIGN OF
    JESUS   85
    A. THE WORLD IS CHANGED   86
    B. GOOD NEWS OF THE MILLENNIAL
       KINGDOM   87
    C. WHO WILL REIGN WITH JESUS?   89
    D. ALL WILL COME AND WORSHIP   90
    E. A TIME OF PROSPERITY AND JUSTICE   90

13. A TIME OF JUDGEMENT   92
    A. SATAN RELEASED FROM THE ABYSS   92
    B. SATAN FORMS AN ARMY   92
    C. GOD PROTECTS HIS OWN   92
    D. SATAN INTO THE LAKE OF FIRE   93

14. GREAT WHITE THRONE JUDGEMENT   94
    A. CHRISTIANS ARE EXEMPT   95
    B. DEEDS AND WORKS JUDGED   96
    C. THE LAMB'S BOOK OF LIFE   96
    D. GUILTY INTO THE LAKE OF FIRE   98

15.	THE KINGDOM OF GOD	99
	A. THE NEW JERUSALEM	99
	B. NOTHING IMPURE WILL ENTER	102
	C. THE HOLY SPIRIT WILL FLOW	103
	D. JESUS SAYS COME	104
16.	ENCOURAGEMENT AND CONCLUSION	106
	A. OPEN YOUR HEART TO JESUS	109
	B. BEING OF SERVICE TO GOD	112
	C. BLESSED BY GOD	112
	D. SHARE WHAT YOU KNOW	113

CHAPTER ONE
INTRODUCTION

We are not expected to live our life without guidance and knowledge of the future. The Master Architect of the universe desires that we all know His plan for the future and the coming events that affect our lives and the lives of others. His plan is revealed in the book 'GREATER THINGS TO COME'. The plan is for all who have been created to live their lives according to God's purpose. The future is revealed to those who will read, learn and apply what is written in this book in order to improve their lives and help others. This book is a simplified but profound version of coming events as prophesied in the Bible, the inerrant word of God.

You determine your destiny. The future is in your hands. Making the right decisions while on the earth ensures you a place in paradise.

This book is unique in that it puts the events that are about to happen in the order in which they will take place. No other book does this.

A. COMING EVENTS PROPHESIED

Daniel 12:4, "But you, Daniel, close up and seal the words of the scroll until the time of the end. Many will go here and there to increase knowledge."

We are living in the 'time of the end'. The words of the scroll have been opened to us. God tells us, through Daniel, that there will be an increase in travel. No longer riding on horses and camels, but flying in jets and rockets that take us into outer space and to the moon.

God also tells us there will be an increase in knowledge. We are in a digital knowledge and information explosion. Highly technical and advancing rapidly in many sectors. What you buy today will often be obsolete in a year or even a few months.

The three thousand or more prophecies in the Bible have been fulfilled, as have all prophecies, except those for the end times.

We are told in Matt. 24:24 that there will be false prophets and teachers in the end times. "false prophets and teachers will appear and deceive even the elect." Everyone must check out the source of all teaching. The true source of prophetic knowledge is the Bible, our manual for living.

The prophecy in the book, GREATER THINGS TO COME, is prophecy inspired by the word of God. Much of this prophecy has been sealed up to be revealed at the time of the end. We are living in that time.

> Revelation 19:10, "For the testimony of
> Jesus is the Spirit of prophecy."

> Isaiah, 46:10, God says, "I have made
> known the end from the beginning."

The Creator of the universe is saying, "In my holy word, I have made known what happened at the beginning and what will happen in the future, in the end times." It is all according to the universal plan for man's salvation.

This book tells where we are now and where we are going according to the word of God in prophecy. The events are written in the order in which they will happen. In order to do so, I have taken prophecies from the Old Testament books of Genesis to Zechariah, primarily the books of Daniel and Ezekiel; and the New Testament books from Matthew to Revelation. I have placed them in chronological order to help readers understand what will happen and when it will happen throughout the coming age.

Through knowledge and understanding of prophecy we become aware of the universal plan of the Creator and are given the option to participate in this great and glorious plan or refuse to participate at our peril.

The Bible tells us we will live forever and forever.

A Christian wrote, "Eternity is in the hearts of mankind." All of mankind, deep down, desires to live forever.

To make the most of today, keep eternity in mind. Always be aware of where you want to end up. Stay on the path that leads to eternity with Jesus the Christ and God Almighty.

> Ecclesiastes 3:11, "He (God) has put
> eternity in their hearts."

This book reveals what will happen from now to eternity.

The question every human must answer is, 'Where will I spend eternity?'

It all depends on how you live your life on earth at this time. What gods and idols you worship. God is a jealous god and demands all of our love and worship.

> Revelation 22:12, Jesus says, "I am coming soon. My reward is with me, and I will give to everyone according to what he has done."

According to what we have done for others, for the church ,the Body of Christ and done to bring glory to God our heavenly Father.

B. FUTURE EVENTS REVEALED

Our purpose is to study things that will happen, the final events of this present age and the last events of sacred history that are beyond this life. The question is, "Where are we going and how will we get there?" This has been a mystery throughout the ages but the answers are given in this book.

> Joel 2:17, "In the last days, God says, "I will pour out my Spirit on all people, Your sons and daughters will prophesy, your young men will see visions. Your old men will dream dreams"

All these phenomena; prophesying, visions and dreams are guided by the Holy Spirit according to the will of God Almighty for our spiritual development.

The Bible, the inerrant word of God, is filled with prophesies, visions and dreams as they are crucial to our understanding the mysteries of God and future events.

The mystery of the future involves the Church and the coming of the Messiah, Jesus the Christ for His true believers. God's promises involve redemption and salvation made possible through the death and resurrection of Jesus the Christ. Whereby, our sins are forgiven, death is overcome, the curse is removed, by His wounds we are healed and we become friends with God.

This generation has been predicted to witness the coming of the Lord when He comes to take His chosen ones with Him before the throne of God in heaven. We will then be with the Lord forever and forever.

The Bible tells of the Kingdom of God and the coming Kingdom where Jesus will rule and reign for one-thousand years.

Every moment of our life brings us closer to the Kingdom of God. The church, Christ's body on earth, the believers, already enjoy certain powers of the kingdom age and the world to come. Jesus told Peter, His disciple:

> Matthew 16:19, "I will give you the keys to the Kingdom."

Jesus desires to give the Keys to the Kingdom to all who have a loving and intimate relationship with Him and His Father.

> Hebrews 6:5, "We ... who have tasted the heavenly gift, who have shared in the Holy Spirit, who have tasted the Word of God and the powers of the coming age ... ."

As you read this book, you will taste the heavenly gift that has been promised to those who understand the mysteries and believe the truth of prophecy. The powers of the coming age will become real and will transform your life.

In the last days, God will speak to us by His precious Son:

> Hebrews 1:2, "... but in these last days, God has spoken to us by His Son, whom he appointed heir of all things and through whom he made the universe."

CHAPTER TWO
PROPHECIES FOR OUR TIME
PROPHECIES OF CHRIST'S LIFE ON EARTH AND HIS RETURN ACCORDING TO THE OLD TESTAMENT

God has not kept us and our ancestors in the dark regarding the sending of His Son to the earth to redeem mankind for the Kingdom of God. Many prophets have spoken about the Son of God appearing in the clouds and then coming to the earth to set up His Millennial Kingdom.

A. PROPHESY REGARDING CHRIST'S FIRST COMING TO EARTH

Isaiah prophesied that Jesus would come, born of a virgin, born in a manger, born not of royalty. The first time God sent His Son as the suffering servant, the Lamb of God, not the deliverer of Israel as some believed He would be.

> Isaiah 7:14, "Therefore the Lord himself will give you a sign: the virgin will be with child and will give birth to a son, and you will call him Immanuel."

The angel Gabriel, God's messenger, told Mary the mother of Jesus to name her son Jesus as he will be Immanuel, which means God with us, the Saviour of the world.

> Luke 1:32, "He will be great and will be called the Son of the Most High."

The angel went on to tell her that the Lord God will put Him on the Throne of David and He will reign over the House of Jacob, and his kingdom will never end.

Everything the Lord has predicted has come true except for the end time prophecies which are explained in the book, 'Greater Things to Come'.

Why Greater Things to Come? It is because God has planned great things for those who worship and praise His Holy name. Greater things are promised for those who exalt Him and sacrifice their bodies and their minds to Him. These greater things are for those who have a loving relationship with His Son, Jesus the Christ.

Who will inherit these greater things? Those who fear the Lord and are filled with joy and peace. Those who are eagerly awaiting the return of Jesus who is coming for His own. Those who love Him and are part of the Church, His body on the earth will inherit the greater things.

> 2 Timothy 4:8, Paul says, "Now there is in store for me the crown of righteousness, which the Lord, the righteous Judge, will award me on that day - and not only to me, but also to all who have longed for his appearing."

Who will receive the crown of righteousness? All who long for the appearing of the Lord Jesus Christ to come for His bride, the church, and take it to heaven.

The prophet Isaiah, 700 years before Jesus came to earth, was told by God what would happen when his Son Jesus came to the earth.

Isaiah tells how Jesus will rule and reign in the Millennial Kingdom.

> God told Isaiah, 9:6, "... and the government will be on His shoulders."

As you read the book you will understand this prophecy. Jesus will be King and rule over the world during His Millennial reign, (one thousand years) and then forever. The government will be on His shoulders as He is governing the world and the universe.

God also tells Isaiah what Jesus the Christ will be called:

> Isaiah 9:6b, "And He, (Jesus the Christ) will be called Wonderful Counsellor, Mighty God, Everlasting Father, Prince of Peace ... He will

reign on David's throne ... establishing and
upholding it with justice and righteousness."

B. JESUS COMING AS KING

Other prophets of the Old Testament also predicted the Lord as the coming King of kings and that his name will be glorified on the earth.

Zechariah 14:9, "The Lord will be king over
the whole earth. On that day there will be
one Lord and His name the only name."

Jeremiah 10:10, "But the Lord is the true God;
he is the living God, the eternal King.

Ezekiel 37:22, "I will make them one nation
in the land, on the mountains of Israel. There
will be one king over all of them ..."

In order to make prophecy come true, the nation of Israel had to be restored to its rightful owners, the descendants of Abraham and Jacob; the Jews and the Israelites. Many of the Prophets of old prophesied that God would return the Israelites to their own land.

Ezekiel 36:24, God says, "I will take you out of the
nations. I will gather you from all the countries and
bring you back into your own land. I will sprinkle
clean water on you and you will be clean."

We know that Israel became a nation in May 1948. The previous Israelite and Jewish inhabitants of Israel were scattered throughout many nations of the world for two thousand five hundred and thirty four years (2534 years). In 1967 the Jews who had returned to Israel, conquered and now live in their capital city Jerusalem, God's royal city. They live in many parts of Israel.

God wants to wash away the grit and grime and cleanse his chosen ones. Never again to have them live in a foreign country, but live in their promised land flowing with milk and honey. A land where God will set up His holy City.

As you read the book you will see how God protects those He loves.

CHAPTER THREE
THE APPEARING OF JESUS CHRIST FOR HIS CHURCH

'A' THE NATURE OF HIS APPEARING

John, the disciple of Jesus, wrote:

> 1 John 2:18, "Dear children this is the last hour, and you have heard that the anti-christ is coming ..."

Now is the last hour for the church, which will be taken up with Jesus and be before the throne of God at the Rapture. The Bible tells us that Jesus will return as He promised. Jesus told his disciples before he ascended to heaven:

> John 14:2a, "I am going there (to heaven) to prepare a place for you, I will come back and take you to be with me that you may know where I am."

The Christians, who are ready and waiting for His return, will be taken by Jesus to be protected in heaven during the seven years of tribulation on the earth.

It also tells us that Jesus and the church will come back to the earth to rule and reign in the Millennial Kingdom. He promises us that for eternity we will be with Him and His Father in the New heaven and the New earth.

This book is written with the belief that Christ's coming to take the church, the true believers to heaven, will be at pre-tribulation (before tribulation). Why?

> Revelation 3:10, "Since you (Christians) have kept my command to endure patiently, I will keep you from the hour of trial that is going to come upon the whole world to test those who live on the earth."

The 'hour of trial' are the seven years of tribulation. A time of testing for the Jews and for those who do not believe in the deity and sanctity of Jesus the Christ. It is a second chance for Jews and all inhabitants on earth to make a decision to follow Jesus the Christ and be saved.

Mid-tribulation and Post-tribulation have been considered for the Rapture, but they are not credible alternatives given scriptural interpretation.

> Titus 2:12 "...live self-controlled, upright and godly lives in this present age, while we wait for the blessed hope, the glorious appearing of our great God and Saviour Jesus the Christ."

> James 5:7, "Be patient, then brothers, until the Lord's coming."

James, the brother of Jesus, tells us to be patient as we wait. He knows that God wants all he has created and chosen to come into His kingdom. He wants all the children of God to be with Him for eternity. God desires a big family to love and care for, which includes everyone who reads this book.

> 1 Thess 1:9, "... wait for God's Son from heaven, whom He raised from the dead - Jesus who rescues us from the coming wrath."

The key words are 'wait' and 'wrath'. We must wait for Jesus, the blessed hope. Wait for His appearing to all on earth. Then He will take His church to be with Him into heaven. Jesus will appear but He will not set foot on the earth at this time.

Wait for God's Son who will rescue us from the coming wrath of God, the tribulation, which will be poured out on those who will not accept Jesus as Lord and God as the Almighty creator.

> 1Peter 1:5, "... an inheritance kept in heaven for you, who through faith are shielded by God's power until the coming of salvation that is ready to be revealed in the last time."

Faith is our shield, which is given us by the power of God. It keeps us safe as we wait for the Lord Jesus to come from heaven and take us to where he is. Our faith and hope are only in God who works supernaturally in our lives and brings us salvation.

> 1 Peter 1:21, "Through Jesus you believe in God, who raised Him from the dead and glorified Him, and so your faith and hope is in God."

> Jude 21; "Keep yourselves in God's love as you wait for the mercy of our Lord Jesus Christ to bring you eternal life."

What is coming next? What must we look for at this time?

B. THE SIGNS OF HIS APPEARING

Jesus tells us to look for the signs and wait for His coming. He does not want us to be surprised and in shock. When the disciples were with Jesus on the Mount of Olives they asked Him:

> Matt. 24:3, "Tell us", they asked, "when will this happen and what will be the sign of your coming at the end of the age?"

Matthew tells us that Jesus told His disciples, and us today, not to be deceived as many will come in His name. He told them they will hear of wars and rumours of wars but such things must happen. However, it is not the end.

Nation will rise against nation and kingdom against kingdom. There will be famines and earthquakes in various places, pestilences and signs in the sky.

Christians will be hated by all nations. Many false prophets will arise and deceive many. There will be wickedness which will turn many away from His love. All this is to happen just before Jesus comes and reveals Himself to the world.

In Luke 21, Jesus gives more signs; fearful events and signs from heaven, the seas and the waves roaring (Floods, tsunamis, hurricanes, tornadoes). Nations will be in anguish and perplexity. The heavenly bodies will be shaken.

Today, many nations are in a time of peril and disruption. Suicide bombers killing innocent people and killing their own relatives and countrymen. Terrorists blowing up buildings and the infrastructure. Pirates capturing unarmed ships and sea going vessels, holding crews and ships for ransom. Young men killing each other (targeted killings) over drugs and money. Drug cartels terrorizing countries. Economies failing, the threat of inflation and deflation. Nations in distress as predicted just before Jesus will return for His chosen ones.

C. MANKIND'S ATTITUDE JUST BEFORE CHRIST'S RETURN

Paul tells in his letter to Timothy, what people will be like just before the return of Jesus the Christ for the true believers:

> Timothy 3:1-5 "There will be terrible times in the last days. People will be lovers of themselves, lovers of money, boastful, proud, abusive, disobedient to their parents, ungrateful, unholy, without love, unforgiving, slanderous, without self control, brutal, treacherous, rash, conceited, lovers of pleasure not lovers of God."

Jesus told us just before he returned for His bride, the church, it would be as in the days of Noah.

> Matthew 24:37, Jesus says, "As it was in the days of Noah, so will it be at the coming of the Son of Man."

People eating and drinking, getting married up to the day Noah entered the ark. Then the floods came and destroyed them all.

Today, many people are living self centred lives which exclude God and Jesus the Christ. Life is lived without giving thanks to God for His provision and protection. Just as in the times of Noah.

What were people like at the time of Noah?

Genesis 6:5, "The Lord saw how great man's wickedness
on the earth had become, and that every inclination of
the thoughts of his heart was only evil all the time."

Genesis 6:11, "Now the earth was corrupt in
God's sight and was full of violence."

We read of this violence and corruption in the world today. The time is near for the return of our Lord and Saviour. Jesus wants us to be aware of the signs of His coming. Make a check list of the signs, as given, and compare it with what is actually happening in the world at this time.

D. THE APPEARING OF CHRIST

Mark 13:24, "But in those days following the
distress, the sun will be darkened, and the moon
will not give its light: the stars will fall from the
sky, and the heavenly bodies will be shaken...."

Just before Christ's return for the redeemed, the sun will be darkened and it will not give its light or its warmth. Power surges and solar flares from the sun will disrupt communications and electronic devices. The moon will not be visible and its pull on the earth will be diminished, which will affect the tides and marine life.

The tropics will cool down and cause many who are unprepared to live in a cold climate, to suffer. The stars will fall and streak across the darkened sky. There will be peals of thunder and flashes of lightening as the heavenly bodies the planets, stars and galaxies are shaken.

God is a mighty God and He will let people know that a great event is about to take place. It is the return of His only begotten Son who will come with the clouds and a multitude of angels.

Matt.24:30b, "At that time... They will see
the Son of Man (Jesus) coming on the clouds
of the sky, with power and great glory."

> Luke 21:28, "When these things begin to
> take place, stand up and lift up your heads,
> because your redemption is drawing near."

Jesus is coming to redeem from the earth those he has paid a great price for with His shed blood on the cross. Those who are ready and eagerly awaiting His return so they can go to heaven.

Men, women and children will see the Son of Man (Jesus) coming on clouds with great glory. Appearing to all on the earth.

> Matt 24:27, " For as lightning that comes
> from the east is visible even in the west, so
> will be the coming of the Son of Man."

> Matt 24:30, "At that time the sign of the
> Son of Man will appear in the sky, and all
> the nations on earth will mourn."

They will see the Son of Man, Jesus the Christ in His glory . Everyone on earth will see Him and will hear Him proclaim that He is the Messiah they have been waiting for. He will show them the nail holes in his hands and feet. They will know that He is truly the Messiah, the Son of God.

Those who have not accepted Him as their Lord and Saviour will mourn because they know they were wrong in rejecting His love, and not bowing to Him and worshipping and thanking Him for what He did for them on the cross.

E. THE RAPTURE OF THE CHURCH

> Matt 24:30, "And He will send His angels with a loud
> trumpet call, and they will gather his elect from the
> four winds, from one end of the heavens to the other."

Believers will be gathered by the angels and taken to Jesus, who will take them before the throne of God.

> 1 Thess 4:16-17 "... the dead in Christ shall rise first (to be with the Lord) and we who are still alive will be caught up together with them in the clouds to meet the Lord in the air. And we will be with the Lord forever."

In order for the chosen ones to be with Jesus before the throne of God, they will have to be in their resurrection bodies as our old bodies won't take such a journey. We are told the trip of trillions of miles will happen in the twinkling of an eye.

> 1 Corinthians 15:42, " The body that is sown perishable, it is raised imperishable."

> 1 Cor. 15:50, "I declare to you, brothers, that flesh and blood cannot inherit the kingdom of God..."

> 1 Cor. 15:52, "... in a flash, in the twinkling of an eye... the dead will be raised imperishable and we will be changed."

> 1 John 3:2, "Dear friends, now we are children of God, and what we will be has not yet been made known. But we know that when He appears, we shall be like Him (Jesus), for we shall see Him as he is."

For Christians, who are the chosen ones, it will be a Hallelujah day. The greatest day of their life. When Jesus appears, we shall see Him in all His glory and honour and in all His majesty and beauty. The greatest news is that we, who love and worship Him, will be like Him.

We know that after Jesus was arrested, falsely accused, beaten and hung on the cross and died, He was placed in a borrowed tomb. Three days later, as He said he would, he arose. The great resurrection of the dead. When women came to the tomb looking for Jesus they did not recognize Him. His disciples saw him in His resurrection body and they too did not recognize Him, until He spoke to them.

When we are in our resurrection, imperishable bodies, I wonder if people will recognize us. I know that Jesus will recognize us and welcome us into the Kingdom.

While the disciples were holed up, with doors barred and windows shuttered, afraid that they too would be crucified, Jesus appeared in their midst. He materialized before their eyes.

I believe that we too, in our bodies like that of Jesus, will be able to materialize anywhere on the earth and in the universe. Walls and bars will not stop us from doing the will of God as we travel throughout the earth and the heavens.

John, the disciple of Jesus the Christ, tells us:

1 John 3:2, "... when He appears, we shall be like Him."

We will have our resurrection bodies for eternity. Whisked off to heaven for the seven years of tribulation and then we will return to the earth with Jesus as King of kings and Lord of lords. The returning believers, who were in heaven, will be coming back to earth as priests and rulers in the Millennial Kingdom. The seventh dispensation.

The believers, who are raptured, are in heaven with Jesus. The church age ends. The dispensation of the church under 'grace by faith' gives way to the fifth dispensation which is the Jews under the 'law of Moses' for the seven years of Tribulation. To be explained later.

CHAPTER FOUR
THE WORLD IN CHAOS

With the Church gone to be with Jesus before the throne of God, there will be chaos on the earth. Nations who hate the Jews will take this opportunity to invade Israel and fulfill a desire to destroy the Jews. A thought which they have expressed openly and harbored for many years.

Nations are in distress at this time

Many Christian world leaders will be taken up at the rapture to be protected by Jesus and His Father in heaven. Christian corporate leaders, who are CEO's of large corporations, will also be taken up along with their Christian employees.

Churches will not open their doors as their leaders and followers are gone to be before the throne of God.

Some Christian Military leaders and police chiefs, along with the Christian rank and file, will be taken up. This leaves gaps in policing and in enforcing the law.

They will all join the millions of believers in heaven, marvelling at the beauty and majesty of the heavens and the universe.

No one to call the shots on earth? Law and Order breaks down.

Ezekiel, the prophet of old, tells what God revealed to him about this time in history.

A. THE INVADING ARMIES FORM

You are advised to READ , Ezekiel Chapters 38 & 39.

> Ezekiel 38:1 "The word of the Lord came to me: Son of Man, set your face against Gog of the land of Magog ...I will turn you around, put hooks in your jaws and bring you with your whole army...In future years, you and many nations will come to the hills of Israel, advancing like a storm, you will be like a cloud covering the land."

Gog is the commander of the Russian Federation and Magog is the land of this federation, which is Russia and its satellite nations.

Summary of Ezekiel, Chapter 38 - God will pull the nations: Russia, Iran, Iraq, Germany, Turkey; North African countries, Libya, Assyria as well as Ethiopia, Sudan and other Arab countries against Israel. To make war with a people living at peace. Living in peace because of the peace treaty that has been signed.

Why will God pull them against Israel?

> Ezekiel 38:16, God says, "I will bring you against
> My land so that the nations will know me when I
> show myself Holy through you before their eyes."

We know that this is not the battle of Armageddon because the combatants are named. At Armageddon, the last big battle at the end of Tribulation, the combatants come from the North, West, East and South.

> Ezekiel 38:7,8, God tells the invading army, "Get ready;
> be prepared, you and the hordes gathered about you,
> and take command of them. After many days you will
> be called to arms. In Future Years you will invade a land
> that has recovered from war, whose people were gathered
> from many nations to the mountains of Israel ..."

We know that this will take place in future years, the end times in which we live. It will happen to a people gathered from many nations. Israel became a nation in 1948 and people have come from all over the world to live in their homeland, their promised land.

It will happen after the rapture of the church.

God has a plan and warns the Jews of this coming invasion. Explained later.

B. SATAN IS THROWN TO EARTH

Before Satan was thrown to the earth, there was a great and wondrous sign that appeared in heaven. Jesus tells us about this sign.

> Revelation 12:1, "A woman clothed with
> the sun, and the moon under her feet, and
> on her head a crown of twelve stars.

To understand who this woman is we have to go back to the book of Genesis.

> Genesis 37:9,10, Joseph told his family, "I had
> another dream, and this time the sun and moon
> and eleven stars bowed down to me."

We know that Jacob, the father of Joseph, was later named Israel. The sun in the dream of Joseph, refers to his father Israel. The moon stands for his mother Rachael. The eleven stars are his eleven brothers. In his dream they all bowed down to him. We know that they did bow down to him in Egypt when he was second in command to Pharaoh.

The twelve stars represent the twelve tribes of Israel. Israel is represented by these celestial signs. Clothed with the sun, with the moon under her feet and a crown of twelve stars on her head.

These twelve stars, the twelve sons of Israel became the twelve tribes of Israel. Which nation was it that God chose to host His Son Jesus the Christ when he came to earth as the deliverer of mankind? It was Israel. Now she, Israel, is pregnant and cries out as birth pangs set in.

> Revelation 12:7, "Then another sign appeared in heaven:
> an enormous red dragon with seven heads and ten horns
> and seven crowns on his heads. His tail swept a third of
> the stars out of the sky and flung them to the earth."

At that time Satan, that old dragon, will fight against Michael the archangel in heaven.

> Revelation 12:7, "And there was war in heaven, Michael
> and his angels fought against the dragon, and the dragon
> and his angels fought back. But he (Satan)was not
> strong enough, and they lost their place in heaven."

Satan will be defeated and thrown down to earth along with his fallen angels.

> Revelation 12:3, "Then another sign appeared in heaven; an enormous red dragon with seven heads and ten horns and seven crowns on his head. His tail swept a third of the stars out of the sky and flung them to the earth."

Note, this is a sign in heaven. We know that the enormous red dragon is Satan, the old devil. The dragon is red because it is covered with the blood of the saints and of God's prophets and people. This passage is a foretelling of the beast, the anti-christ, who is to come. The seven heads are where the beast and Satan will rule. These are the seven hills of Rome. The ten horns are ten kings who will rule the earth under the control of the beast and Satan. The seven crowns on his head signifies that the beast and Satan are scheduled to rule the world for seven years.

Revel. 12:4, Tells us that Satan will bring down with him, to the earth, one third of the angels of heaven. These are the angels who have fallen victim to his lies and deception. Satan and the fallen angels are thrown out of heaven by God Almighty.

> Revelation 12:4b, "The dragon (Satan) stood in front of the woman (Israel) who was about to give birth, so that he might devour her child the moment it was born."

Satan has always been the enemy of all who are related to God Almighty and all who worship Jesus. We are children of God and are not exempt from his deceptions. Now he wants to kill Jesus as he is being born.

> Revelation 12:5, "She gave birth to a son, a male child, who will rule all the nations with an iron sceptre."

We know that this male child is Jesus the Christ. God will have nothing to do with such an evil scheme by his enemy Satan.

> Revelation 12:6, "And her child was snatched up to God and his throne."

Satan comes to kill Jesus the male child who will rule all the nations with an iron sceptre. He will learn that Jesus is in heaven with his heavenly Father protected from his reach. This angers Satan who goes through the nations to look for those who worship God Almighty and Jesus the Christ

C. THE JEWS ARE WARNED PROTECTED BY GOD

Before Satan is thrown down and before the armies invade Israel, God warns the Jews. Israelites see on their surveillance systems the massive armies being formed both in the north and in the south. These armies are moving towards Israel. God prepares an avenue of escape for His people.

> Revel 12: 6, "The woman (Israel), fled into the desert to a place prepared for her by God, where she might be taken care of for 1,260 days."

These three and a half years are the first three and a half years of Tribulation.
How will Israel, the Jews, flee?

> Revel. 12:14, The woman was given the two wings of a great eagle, so that she might fly to a place prepared for her in the desert, where she would be taken care of for three and a half years, out of the serpents reach.

On the wings of a great eagle (American troop carriers?) to a place in the desert where God will take care of His chosen ones, the Jews, for 3 ½ years. Out of the serpent's reach. No one can harm these Jews protected by God Almighty.
What is amazing is that John, the disciple of Jesus, who is recording what he saw and what he heard, sees Jews being transported in large planes.

> Revel. 12:14, The woman (Israel), was given the
> wings of a great eagle, so that she might fly to
> the place prepared for her in the desert ..."

In the first century, John's time, people only dreamed of flying. But he sees large planes with wings of a great eagle (insignia) transporting the Jews to where God will protect them for the first three and a half years of Tribulation.

D. ARMIES GO AGAINST THE JEWS

> Ezekiel 39:2, God says, "... I will bring you from the far
> north and send you against the mountains of Israel."

The Jews who did not get on the troop carriers flee to the hills and mountains of Israel accompanied by the complete Israeli army with all its weaponry.

God prophecies about the army that will pursue the Jews in the mountains.

> Ezekiel 39:3, God says "Then I will strike
> your bow from your left hand and make your
> arrows drop from your right hand."

God is saying that he will disarm the army coming against the Jews in the mountains of Israel. He will utterly destroy this army that dares to attack His people.

> Exekiel 39:4, "On the mountains of Israel you will fall,
> you and all your troops and the nations with you."

While this army is advancing against the Israelis in the hills and mountains, the other half of the army is planning their attack on the Jews in the desert. Going against those whom God is protecting for the first three and a half years of tribulation.

Satan is still upset at the fact he could not kill Jesus the Christ. He sees the massive armies which have invaded the land of Israel.

How large is this army? Many millions.

> Ezekiel 38:16, God says, "You will advance against
> my people Israel, like a cloud that covers the land."

Satan, through one he has indwelt, asks the Palestinians, "Where are the Jews?" The Palestinians tell him, pointing to the South East, "The planes flew that way."

Soviet planes and other aircraft fly over God's no-fly zone to destroy the Jews. Their plane's electrical systems fail and they crash. Armoured vehicles are abandoned as their computers and electrical systems fail. They won't start.

E. GOD PROTECTS HIS CHOSEN ONES

Satan talks the invading forces into attacking the Jews. He controls the forces of evil as well as the Palestinian men and boys with rocks and weapons as they march out to annihilate the Jews once and for all.

The book of Revelation has symbols which we must understand . When it speaks of seas, waters and rivers, it can mean "nations, peoples and multitudes."

> Revelation 17:15, "Then the angel said to me, "the waters
> you saw ... are peoples, multitudes, nations and languages."

> Revelation 17:1, "Come, I will show you the punishment
> of the great prostitute , who sits on many waters."

The prostitute is the false religious order which has power over many regions of the earth; peoples, nations, multitudes and tribes. She is not sitting on waters, but rather she is monitoring many nations and peoples over which she has control.

> Revel 13:1 "And I saw a beast coming out of the sea."

The beast is coming out of the nations to rule the earth for three and a half years. He is not coming out of the Mediterranean Sea or any body of water.

> Revel. 12:15, "Then from his mouth, the serpent (Satan) spewed water like a river, (sent the military forces marching across the land to battle) to overtake the woman Israel, (the Jews) and sweep her away with the torrent. (destroy God's people)."

> Psalm 83:4 "Come they say, let us destroy them as a nation, that the name of Israel will be remembered no more."

At the time of David, the enemies of Israel wanted to destroy the Jews. This hatred is still evident today among nations and peoples. Antisemitism.

Satan orders the army into action and they march towards where they have calculated the Jews are being cared for by God Almighty.

> Rev. 12:16, "But the earth opened its mouth swallowing the river (army) that the dragon spewed out of his mouth." (Sent into battle)

God causes an earthquake which creates a crevice, a large crack in the earth. The whole army tumbles into this huge hole. God caves in the walls of the surrounding cliffs and buries the invading armies.

Ezekiel tells us that God will also intervene on the mountains of Israel.

> Ezekiel 39:7, "I will make known my holy name among the people of Israel. I will no longer let my Holy name be profaned, and the nations will know that I am the Lord the Holy One of Israel."

> Ezekiel 39:11 "On that day I will give Gog (the Russian leader) and his army, a burial place in Israel..."

> Ezekiel 39:9, " For seven years the people of Israel will use the weapons of the defeated enemy for fuel."

Both the army that invaded the Israelites on the mountains and hills of Israel and the army that marched against the Israelites in the desert are defeated by God, supernaturally.

The few that escape flee the country and run back home.

Satan could not kill Jesus or the Israelites, the Jews. This angers him.

> Revel 12:17, "Then the Dragon (Satan) was enraged at the Woman, (Israel, the Jews) and went off to make war against the rest of her offspring -those who obey God's commandments and hold to the testimony of Jesus." (The Christians).

Christians are now Satan's target to be killed. To be wiped off the face of the earth. Those who hold to the testimony of Jesus the Christ our redeemer and our Saviour.

F. THE BEAST APPEARS

With the Jews safe and the remaining armies retreated from Israel, Satan, that old Dragon will look to the nations, the European Union, the Revived Roman Empire, for the beast. The anti-christ, known as the beast, will receive Satan's power to rule the earth.

> Revel 13:1 "And the dragon stood on the shore of the sea (nation). And I saw a beast coming out of the sea (the nations). He had ten horns (kings) and seven heads (where he will reign), with ten crowns on his horns, and on each head a blasphemous name."

Words in brackets are mine as explanations of the content. Seven heads are where Satan and the beast will set up their kingdom. These are the seven hills of Rome. They will rule from the city of Rome in Italy.

Ten crowns mean that the beast, Satan and ten kings will conquer and will rule the earth. Blasphemous names mean that the beast will come against and profane the saints, God Almighty and His son Jesus the Christ

> Revel 13:2b, "The dragon (Satan) gave the beast his power and his throne and his authority."

CHAPTER FIVE
BEFORE TRIBULATION

A. A PEACE TREATY FOR SEVEN YEARS

For many years the world leaders of our time have tried to broker a peace treaty between Israel and the Palestinians. None have been able to do so as it has not been according to God's will and God's timing.

But the Book of Daniel tells us there will be a peace treaty signed before the rapture of the church. There will be a peace treaty signed for 7 years.

> Daniel 9:27. "He will confirm a covenant, with many, for 7 years."

> Ezekiel 38:8, "In future years you will invade a land (Israel) that has recovered from war."

The only way Israel will recover from war will be if a peace treaty is signed. This peace treaty has been predicted and it will happen. People will celebrate as they believe there will be no more wars and all will be well on planet earth for at least seven years.

B. JEWISH TEMPLE IS REBUILT IN JERUSALEM

The returning Jews from the hills and mountains of Israel will build their temple in Jerusalem. They will worship and make daily sacrifices. How do we know they will build the temple?

> Daniel 9:27, " In the middle of the 'seven' (7 years of Tribulation) he (the anti-christ, the beast) will put an end to sacrifice and offering. And on the wing of the temple..."

There has to be a temple in Jerusalem in order for the beast to put his image in 'the wing of the temple.' There also has to be a temple in order to make sacrifices and offerings.

We know that the Jews are yearning to build their temple. When the Palestinian men and boys are buried, as they pursue the Jews in the desert, there will be little opposition to the building of the temple at the beginning of Tribulation. As well, there will be a peace treaty signed for seven years which protects the Jews.

C. 144,000 SERVANTS OF GOD ISRAELI EVANGELISTS

God always has a presence on the earth. Just before tribulations begins, God will reveal His 144,000 'servants of God' to take the place of the raptured Church, who were His presence on the earth for over 2000 years.

These are Israeli evangelists who will be God's presence on earth for the first three and a half years of Tribulation. They are sealed by God for their protection.

> Revel 7:3, "Do not harm the land or the sea or the trees, until we put a seal on the foreheads of the servants of God."

This is a seal of protection, as these servants of God are vulnerable to attack from Satan and the forces of evil. These servants will go first of all to the Jews and then to the Gentiles throughout the world proclaiming the Gospel of God . They will then be with Jesus, redeemed from the earth, after three and a half years. They will be taken up at the second harvest of believers before mid-tribulation.

These servants of God from the twelve tribes of Israel have to contend daily and hourly with the apostate religious order, which is out to destroy and annihilate them. These evangelists help new converts to Christianity, by teaching them and by helping them to avoid the forces out to persecute them. They are the ones who have not taken the mark of the beast to buy and sell and have not bowed to the image of the beast, but now bow to Jesus, their redeemer and saviour.

Only God knows who belongs to each of the twelve tribes of Israel as these tribes have been scattered to the four corners of the earth during the Assyrian and Babylonian invasions.

The Jews were also scattered when their temple was burned and destroyed by the Romans. This caused the Jews to be dispersed among the nations.

These 144,000 are from all nations of the world, the twelve lost tribes of Israel.

What is the criteria?

> Revelation 14:4, "These are those who did not defile themselves with women, for they kept themselves pure.

These men are celibate and in union with Jesus the Christ. To have sex before marriage is a form of spiritual defilement, fornication. Sex after marriage is a holy act of joining a man with a woman together making them one body. It is not a form of defilement.

The other criteria is that they, 'kept themselves pure'. We too must keep ourselves pure and attain to holiness and live a godly life, as we wait for the Lord to come and take us before the throne of God.

Jesus and God are, at this present time, preparing these 144,000 for the task of being servants of God. They are being taught to preach the gospel of God and bring converts into the Kingdom.

D. GOD'S ANGEL PROCLAIMS THE GOSPEL

An angel flies in midair proclaiming to every nation, language and people:

> Revel. 14:6,7 "Fear God and give Him glory, because the hour of judgement has come. Worship Him who made the heavens and the earth, the sea and the springs of water."

This is the first of three angels flying in mid air who will speak to people in every corner of the earth in their own language and dialect. To every nation, tribe, language and people.

No one will be able to say they did not hear the message of God for salvation proclaimed to the earthly inhabitants just before Tribulation.

People on earth at that time include those who have been to church and those who have been involved in some aspect of the body of Christ and have heard God's message of salvation, but they did not respond. They went back to their earthly ways and old life style.

They were not being filled with the Holy Spirit and daily praising and thanking Jesus for what He did on the cross. Not exalting God Almighty and thanking Him for sending His Son to go to the cross and shed His blood for the forgiveness of our sins.

They now hear an angel proclaiming the gospel. They know that many Christians who belonged to the church are no longer on the earth. They were told Jesus was coming for those who were ready but they ignored the message and continued in their disobedience. Refusing to maintain a spiritual relationship with God and Jesus the Christ.

NOW, they hear an angel of God proclaiming the message of salvation:

> Revelation 14:6 "fear God and give Him glory.
> Because the hour of judgement has come."

Their conscience clicks in and they take the message seriously. They hear about a meeting of Christians led by two or three of the 144,000, who are bringing people into the kingdom. They want to know more about the "hour of judgement." Their question is, "Will I be judged and how can I avoid this judgement?"

This is a question everyone who reads this book might ask.

Read on, the answers are given.

E. THE SEVEN SEALED SCROLL

Revelation, chapter five tells of the seven sealed scroll which is held in the right hand of God Almighty.

John, the apostle of Jesus, stood weeping because no one was found worthy to open the scroll. The elders assured John that one is worthy.

They told him it is none other than the Lion of the Tribe of Judah, the promised deliverer and redeemer of mankind, Jesus the Christ.

The only one worthy to open the seals is Jesus the Messiah. Rev.5:6-7. Why? Because He came to earth as our Redeemer and Saviour, as Immanuel, God with us. Jesus earned this right by sacrificing his life for us.Rev 5:9b, "You (Jesus) are worthy to take the scroll and open its seals, because you were slain, and with your blood you purchased men for God. You have made them to be a kingdom and priests to serve God and they will reign on the earth."

God tells us what Christians, the true believers, will do throughout eternity. They will serve God Almighty and reign upon the earth according to His will.

The scroll God handed to Jesus has writings on both sides. On one side is the 'Title Deed' to the earth and on the other side are the 'Judgements' that will be meted out on the world in the last half of Tribulation. These judgements are often severe and extremely painful.

F. WHY 7 YEARS OF TRIBULATION

Why does the Tribulation last for seven years? Who is the Tribulation for?

Daniel 9:24-26, "Seventy - sevens are decreed for your people and your holy city to finish transgressions, to put an end to sin, to atone for wickedness, to bring in everlasting righteousness, seal up vision and prophecy and to anoint the Most Holy."

Seventy- (sevens) are 490 years which were allocated by God, through Darius, the king of Babylon. It is for the captured Jews to go back to Jerusalem and rebuild their temple, put an end to sin (which they did not do), atone for wickedness (which did not happen), bring in everlasting righteousness (that is not complete), seal up vision and prophecy (which is still with us today), and they were to anoint the Most Holy One, Jesus the Christ.

Instead, they crucified Jesus the Christ before His ministry was completed.

They were to worship their God and host Jesus our Lord and Saviour. They were also to anoint Him as King of kings and Lord of lords. It didn't happen.

In Bible prophecy, the years planned for the Jews to return to Israel and for Jesus the Christ to complete His ministry was 490 years. The dispensation of the Jews under the Law. Jesus did not complete His ministry. He was cut off by being severely beaten, nailed to a cross, killed and buried in a borrowed tomb.

> Daniel 9:25,26 "There will be seven- sevens and sixty- two sevens ... the anointed one (Jesus), will be cut off and will have nothing."

Jesus did not have a chance to fulfill His purpose as given in Daniel 9:24 as explained above.7x7 =49, plus 62x7=434 ** total 483 years. Seven years short of the promised 490 years given by God. Short 7 years under the Law for the Jews as promised.

When Jesus established the Church, His body on earth, the dispensation of the Law ended, (the law given to Moses). The dispensation of Grace by faith as instituted by Jesus the Christ came into effect. We are in this 6th dispensation.

These seven years promised to the Jews are seven years under the law to be carried out during the Tribulation. God never breaks a promise and He promised 490 years to the Jews. They will receive these 7 years under the law as a time of Tribulation, a time of testing, trial and temptation.

Primarily, the first three and a half years of Tribulation are for the Jews and the Israelites who were under the law of Moses.

The Tribulation is also for those Gentiles who were not ready when Jesus came to harvest the earth at the rapture of the church. The believers, who were ready and waiting, have been taken with Jesus to be before the throne of God. Those who were not ready have been left behind. But there is still hope.

God gives all on earth a second and even a third or fourth chance to come and be saved. But at some point, God will say, enough is enough.

> Revel. 22:10,11, "Do not seal up the words of the prophecy of this Book,(Revelation) because the time is near. Let him who does wrong, continue to do wrong; let him who is vile, continue to be

> vile; (filthy) let him who does right, continue to do
> right; let him who is holy, continue to be holy."

At some point in time, we will not be able to change our behaviour and our character. When we die, there will be no chance of changing and becoming either right or holy, as the case might be. Some people teach that persons can change after death, but Jesus refutes that claim. Let him who .... continue to be ....

This is their character and behaviour throughout life. People will be judged according to their character, their life-style and their actions while on the earth. Whatever you sow that is what you will reap.

> Galatians 6:17, "Do not be deceived: God cannot be
> mocked. A man reaps what he sows. The one who
> sows to please his sinful nature, from that nature
> he will reap destruction; the one who sows to please
> the Spirit, from that Spirit will reap eternal life.

That is why, if we desire to change and become holy, the time is now. Why? As it says, "the time is near." It will be too late after you die.

Then you will either be with the Lord forever or cast out of His presence into outer darkness or worse.

You will be either in the wrong, because you did not have your sins forgiven and you allowed Satan to control your life. Or, because of your sinful nature and your wicked behaviour, you will be classified as a vile and a filthy person.

Some will be known as one who is right and good. A law abiding citizen but not righteous in the sight of God, because you will not let Jesus come into your life and forgive your sins and wrap you in the robe of righteousness. Being good is not good enough to get into the kingdom of God.

The ultimate is to be Holy, worthy to be with God and Jesus in the coming New Jerusalem. Praising God and Jesus the Christ continually.

As Tribulation begins, God raises up 144,000 evangelists from the twelve tribes of Israel who will go throughout the earth, first to the Jews then to the Gentiles, teaching, witnessing, discipling and bringing them into a relationship with Jesus the Christ and God the Father..

Protecting converts from the false prophet who demands that they take the mark of the beast and bow to his image. It is a task only these 144,000 can carry out as they are trained by the best teachers in the universe; God Almighty, Jesus the Christ and the Holy Spirit.

Keeping these converts safe from the false religious order is a great feat as these 'servants of God' are hounded mercilessly by the members of the false religious order, who are a bunch of demon possessed, blood thirsty, evil spirited men and women.

Tribulation is often called the time of Jacob's trouble. Jacob representing the Jews. It is also a time of trouble for those who were not ready when Jesus returned for His Bride, the Church, at the Rapture.

During the first half of Tribulation these newly converted Christians desire to bask in Christ's love and be in union with our Lord and Saviour. They desire to be prepared to become servants of God Almighty in the coming New Jerusalem.

The second half of Tribulation is when God will vent His wrath on those who will not worship Him and bow the knee to Jesus Christ His Son. This time of Great Tribulation is for those who killed and shed the blood of His saints and prophets; those who will not repent of their evil ways, corrupt desires and bad behaviour.

It is a time of judgement on those who deny the Sovereignty of God and His Son Jesus the Christ.

CHAPTER SIX
FIRST HALF of TRIBULATION BEGINS WHICH LASTS FOR THREE AND A HALF YEARS

A. THE BEAST COMES TO POWER

> Rev 13:1-10 "And the dragon (Satan)
> stood on the shore of the sea."

What is he looking for? Satan is looking for the 'beast' the antichrist, to gain control over the nations. Sea is 'water' which stands for nations, multitudes and peoples. Satan is looking to the nations of the earth for the beast. The dragon, Satan, finds the one he has been looking for:

> Revel. 13:2 "The dragon gave the beast his
> power and his throne and great authority."

Authority over the earth which is in chaos, distressed and in perplexity, still suffering economic woes, problems with capitalism, drug abuse and many social and political issues.

The beast deceives the people on earth into believing that he is the saviour of the world. Once again imitating Jesus, who is the true Saviour of the world. The beast is telling all on earth that he has solutions to every one of their problems. Only God Almighty has the solutions to all our problems. We only have to ask and receive, according to God's will, and He will solve our problems and give us a blessing.

> Revelation 13:4, "Men worshipped the dragon
> because he had given authority to the beast,
> and they also worshipped the beast."

On earth we now have Satan worship and beast worship

> Revel 13:8, "All inhabitants of the earth will worship the beast-all whose names have not been written in the Lamb's Book of Life."

B. DECEPTION OF THE BEAST

The beast is fatally wounded in the head.

> Revel. 13:3, "One of the heads of the beast seemed to have a fatal wound, but the fatal wound had been healed. The whole world was astonished and followed the beast."

The beast is pronounced clinically dead and on life support. The people mourn as he is their only hope for peace and a future full of promised riches and pleasure.

After three days the fatal wound is healed An imitation of the resurrection of Jesus the Christ after three days in the tomb.

Men admire the beast and Satan.

> Revel.13:5 "The beast was given a mouth to utter proud words and blasphemy and exercised his authority for 42 months." (3 ½ years)

The beast has power and authority for the first three and a half years of tribulation. For the second half of tribulation, the beast loses his power.

C. POWER TO CONQUER CHRISTIANS

> Revel. 13:7 "He was given power to make war against the saints and to conquer them."

The saints are those who have given their life to Jesus the Christ. Many are coming to Christ as a result of their being discipled by some of the 144,000 servants of God.

Others have joined together in house churches.

The church buildings on earth have been taken over by the 'One World Religion,' the apostate religious order. This religious order is known as 'Babylon' because they follow the despicable teachings and observances of Babylon of old.

The saints are arrested and brain washed, tortured and forced to renounce their love for Jesus. They are conquered but not defeated; they belong to Jesus the Christ and many will not make the mistake of turning away from Him again.

They become martyred saints rather than disclaim their love of the Lord.

D. THE FALSE PROPHET COMES

The beast has an accomplice:

> Revel 13:11, " Then I saw another beast, coming out of the earth. He had two horns like a lamb, but he spoke like a dragon (devil) and made the earth and its inhabitants worship the first beast."

He looked like a holy man and is called the false messiah or false prophet, but he speaks like a demon under the control of Satan and the beast. He performs great and miraculous signs deceiving the inhabitants of the earth; bringing fire down from heaven. He orders men to set up images of the beast in every city and town. These images will be set up in the abandoned churches, mosques and temples, now occupied by the false religious order.

If there is not an image available, they have a picture of the beast or a cardboard cut out of his image, which must be bowed to.

In large centres, they set up an image of the beast which can talk, (when asked the right questions), and proclaim how great are Satan, the beast and the false prophet. It causes people to believe that these three actually deserve their worship and honour.

This false prophet controls the false religion and carries out the orders of the beast and of Satan in the affairs of government.

E. MARK OF THE BEAST

Anyone who will not worship the beast and bow to its image and take the mark of the beast on their right hand or forehead is to be imprisoned and tortured. If they will not renounce Jesus as Lord of their life they will be beheaded.

> Revel 13:16, "He also forced everyone small and great, rich and poor free and slave, to receive a mark on his right hand or on his forehead so that no one could buy or sell unless he had the mark of the beast..."

In doing so, Satan, the beast and the false prophet have control over everyone on earth who take the mark. They have control of the government, finances, army and everything that moves and has its being.

God warns people not to take the mark and not to bow to the image of the beast.

F. GOD SENDS AN ANGEL- WARNING

God sends an angel from heaven speaking to every nation in their own language, tongue and dialect.

> Revel 14:9-12- A third angel warns all on earth, "If anyone worships the beast and his image and receives his mark on the forehead or on the hand, he too will drink of the wine of God's fury, which has been poured out full strength into the cup of his wrath. He will be tormented with burning sulphur in the presence of the holy angels and the Lamb...."

God warns everyone on earth. But will they listen? No, they will not.

God warns us that anyone who takes the mark of the beast or bows to the image of the beast will 'drink of God's fury'. I can't think of any fury worse than that of God's fury. God goes on to say that His fury has been 'poured out full strength'. Not just a bit of His fury, but the full strength of His fury. That is potent stuff. If that doesn't scare a person nothing else will. God goes on to say that it is poured into the cup of God's wrath. When we incite God's wrath, we know that the penalty will be severe. Tormented for eternity... in the presence of the holy angels and the Lamb of God.

People have been warned not to take the mark of the beast or bow to his image. They have been warned by God that there will be dire consequences. But many will not listen. They follow the desires of the flesh and the lies of Satan. Those who are ministered to by the 144,000 servants of God and those who are in house churches, will NOT take the mark or bow to the beast or to his image.

Every hour of every day the 144,000 will be encouraging those who will not take the mark of the beast and bow to the image of the beast, to accept Jesus as their Lord and Saviour. If caught, these new believers know that they will be tortured and killed. But their love of Jesus is greater than their fear of torture and death.

God, in His great wisdom, has put His seal of protection on these 144,000 servants of God as they know that if they are caught they will be martyred. They have no fear as God is their shield and their fortress.

The question each person in this situation must answer is, "What will I do?" Bow to Jesus and be saved or bow to the image of the beast, take his mark and be under God's wrath. Cast out of God's presence and into outer darkness or worse. Tormented day and night as they keep reminding themselves that they had the chance of being saved and being in the kingdom of God, but they denied Jesus and refused His call to come and be saved. They declined the call to come and receive His promise of eternal life with Him and His Father.

The answer of what to do is obvious if you want to be in the presence of God and Jesus the Christ forever.

For the first half of Tribulation these 144,000 will be spreading the Word of God, while evading the forces out to destroy them.

G. THE FIRST SEAL IS OPENED BY JESUS

After this, Jesus the Christ will open the first seal of the scroll.

Many theologians and scholars try in vain to explain that the seals are to be opened one after another before the judgements. In fact, the seals are opened during the seven years of Tribulation. The First seal is opened at the beginning of tribulation, but the second and succeeding seals will not be opened until after the second harvest, which happens at Mid-Tribulation.

Why is the second seal not opened until after the first three and a half years of Tribulation? One reason is that there is a peace treaty for seven years signed just prior to the rapture. If the second seal is broken near the beginning of Tribulation that would nullify the peace treaty only months after it was signed, which doesn't make sense and is not predicted. The opening of the Second Seal takes peace from the earth.

> Revelation 6:4 "Then another horse came out, a fiery red one. Its rider was given power to take peace from the earth ..."

Another reason why the remaining seals are not opened until the second half of tribulation is because God is still working in the lives of many on earth during the first half of Tribulation. They are committing their lives to Jesus the Christ.

They don't deserve to be on earth during the Trumpet judgements and the Bowls of God's wrath, which are poured out on those who deny Jesus as Lord . These Trumpet and Bowl judgements are for those who are unrepentant and deny completely the saving power of Jesus. They are for those who have shed the blood of the saints and blasphemed God Almighty and His Son, Jesus the Christ.

Those who desire to be with God and Jesus for eternity during the first half of tribulation will be protected by the servants of God. Others will be killed because of their testimony to Jesus the Christ as Lord of their lives. They have chosen to become martyrs rather than give up their hope in Jesus the Christ.

The Trumpet judgements and bowls of God's wrath are reserved for the Great Tribulation, which are the last three and a half years of tribulation.

Jesus and the 144,000 servants of God are ministering to those who desire to give their life to the Lord and are being prepared for the second harvest.

The First Seal is opened by Jesus the Christ at the beginning of Tribulation.

> Rev. 6:1-2 , "Come! I looked, and there before me was a white horse! Its rider held a bow, and he was given a crown, and he rode out as a conqueror bent on conquest."

When armies on horses conquered a city or province, the king, crowned, rode into town on a white stallion proclaiming victory.

Revel 6:1, This rider on the white horse has no arrows (no ammunition). He has only a bow which means he will win the victory by diplomacy, threats and deception. It also means that he has control over the weapons of war. The crown represents the fact that he will conquer the earth and be king over the earth.

> "...rode out as a conqueror bent on conquest."

A pseudo peace, enforced and demanded, during the first half of tribulation will prevail. The seven years of peace, as proclaimed by Daniel, will last for the first three and a half years of Tribulation and then the treaty (covenant) will be broken.

H. DANIEL'S VISION OF THE BEAST

> Daniel 7:23, this king, (the beast) will, "...devour the whole earth, trampling it down and crushing it."

> Daniel 7:7, sees in a vision the beast, "terrifying and frightening and very powerful. It has large teeth; it crushes and devours its victims and tramples them underfoot ..."

The whole earth is under the control of this wicked beast. He terrifies those who come against him. People are frightened into submission. They observe how the beast, with his police and army crush rebellions and dissenters. No one dares speak against the government, the false religious order or any official.

Daniel 7:23-25 God tells Daniel about this beast. How he will speak against the Most High God and oppress His saints and try to change the set times and laws.

> Daniel 7:25b, "The saints will be handed over to him
> for a time, times and half a time," (3 ½ years)

For a time is one year, times is two years and half a time which adds up three and a half years. The first three and a half years of tribulation the saints will be hunted, tortured and killed.

Jesus also tells us how those who have accepted Him as their Lord and Saviour at this time will be treated during the first three and a half years of Tribulation. They will be hunted and conquered.

> Rev 13:7 "He, the beast. was given power to make war
> against the saints (Christians) and to conquer them."

To make war is to fight against the enemy. In the eyes of the beast and Satan, Christians are the enemy which must be conquered and wiped off the face of the earth. Fortunately, God will have the final say.

> Revel 12:17, "Then the dragon (Satan) went off to make
> war against ... those who obey God's commandments
> and hold to the testimony of Jesus the Christ."

At this time in history both the dragon, Satan and beast are making war against the saints, the chosen ones of God.

I. ONE WORLD GOVERNMENT

During the first year of the reign of the beast, he will set up a one world government controlled by the beast, false prophet and Satan.

It will consist of: one army under the control of the central government, one world justice system including the courts and police force, one monetary currency (control of banks and the world bank). One religious order, Babylon, under the control of the occult, the witches, cults and demons, religions that do not worship Jesus Christ or worship God Almighty.

One language to be spoken throughout the world. Only one nation on earth. One education system which brain washes and indoctrinates children and their parents into Satan worship and worship of the beast and the false prophet. Total control by force and coercion. Everyone must comply to the wishes of the state or be jailed and tortured. If they will not bow and worship the beast they will be killed.

Everything will be controlled by giant computers able to do a trillion calculations a second. Everyone on earth who has the mark of the beast will be tracked throughout the earth. There will be no privacy. People will become robots, controlled in all they do. No freedom of expression will be allowed. There will be ten kings ruling over ten areas of the earth.

> Rev. 17:12, "The ten horns you saw are ten kings, who for one hour will receive authority as kings along with the beast."

J. APOSTATE RELIGIOUS ORDER

READ Revelation, Chapter 17. It tells about the great prostitute who sits on many waters (waters represent nations and peoples). This false religious order will set up its operation throughout the world in every town, village and city. The apostate religion (Babylon) will set up shop in the abandoned churches, synagogues and temples in every region of the earth. They will initiate demonic practices, black magic, sorcery and occultic activities.

The demonic trinity, Satan, the beast and the false prophet will persuade everyone that this is the way to live and enjoy life. The catch is, people have to pay a price to take part in these Satanic practices, which makes this false religious order very rich.

John, the apostle of God , tells us what he observes while monitoring the apostate religious order which is responsible for these carnal and lascivious activities.

> Revel 17:2, "With her (the apostate religion) the kings of the earth committed adultery and the inhabitants of the earth were intoxicated with the wine of her adulteries."

This false religious order has become so appealing to the world that she is able to seduce all ten kings of the world and those in high positions into believing her deceptions and lies. All inhabitants on earth are intoxicated and captivated with this perverted life style. A form of spiritual adultery.

This religious system is controlled and orchestrated by Satan, who is out to destroy all who are created by God Almighty.

> John 8:44, "... He (Satan), was a murderer from the beginning, not holding to the truth, for there is no truth in him. When he lies, he speaks his native language, for he is a liar and the father of lies."

Not only does this harlot, this religious prostitute, charm and seduce the kings, but she also commits spiritual adultery with all the inhabitants of the world. People are intoxicated with her appealing sensual offerings; her glitter and glamour. At this time the beast has ordered everyone in any position to go and have their fortune told at these religious centres all over the earth. As in Babylon, there are temple prostitutes, gambling, drugs and every vice imaginable to mankind. All at a price. The leaders in these centres are fortune tellers, witches, occultists, false religious leaders and followers, cult leaders and followers, demon possessed persons and those with evil spirits.

In this way Satan has control over the people on earth and persons in high positions such as Kings, Generals and Political Officials.

> Rev. 18:2 "She," (this false religion, Babylon) ".has become a home for demons and a haunt for every evil spirit...."

> Revel. 17:3. An angel carries John, in the Spirit, into a desert. There he sees a woman, (representing the false religion) sitting on a scarlet beast, (covered with the blood of the saints). The scarlet beast, representing

> the government, is covered with blasphemous
> names and it has seven heads and ten horns.

The one world religious order is riding on top of the world government. The false religion is running rough shod over the beast and the false prophet. This religious anomaly is now more popular and powerful than the beast and the false prophet.

> Revel 17: 6 "I saw the woman was drunk with
> the blood of the saints, the blood of those
> who bore testimony to Jesus the Christ."

She was riding a scarlet beast, red with the blood of the saints. Those who accepted Christ as their Lord and Saviour were in danger of arrest, torture and death by decapitation.

The apostate demonic religious order cannot co-exist with those who keep the commands of Jesus and love the Lord with all their heart, mind and soul.

This apostate Babylonian religion will exist throughout the world. They demand that people pay a high tax to them and pay to attend and partake of their services. They issue a summons to those who break the law and put the proceeds into the treasury of the apostate religious order.

Some of the services they offer include; witchcraft, fortune telling, the occultic practices of Babylon, temple prostitutes both boys and girls, gambling and revelling, astrology and sorcery, drugs and anything which will arouse the evil desires of the participants. Those things that appeal to the dark side of mankind will be offered by the false religious order.

Christians are warned about such adultery with the world and the worldly. James 4:4, "You adulterous people, don't you know that friendship with the world is hatred toward God? Anyone who chooses to be a friend of the world becomes the enemy of God."

People in those days were worshipping false gods and were caught up in the sinful ways of the world. James, the brother of Jesus, is warning them just as he is warning us in our present generation not to get caught up in the adulterous ways of the world. This is spiritual adultery. Worshipping anything or anyone more that you worship God

Almighty and His Son Jesus the Christ is idolatry, which is a grievous sin.

Many people have the outward form of a Christian but they have no spiritual reality. These are people who are often flirting with the world and its glitter and glamour, then trying to masquerade with religious posturing.

God knows our heart and our mind. This behaviour does not fool our Lord and Saviour. God is not mocked.

Anyone who will not bow to the image of the beast, which was set up in all their places of beast worship and Satan worship throughout the earth, are arrested and brain washed. If they will not deny Jesus as Lord after being tortured, they are beheaded.

> Revel. 6:9, "I saw under the altar the souls of those who had been slain because of the word of God and the testimony they had maintained. They called out in a loud voice. "How long Sovereign Lord, holy and true, until you judge the inhabitants of the earth and avenge our blood?"

They shed their blood while being tortured and beaten and finally beheaded. Why? Because of their love for Jesus their Lord.

They want vengeance for their blood poured out on the ground by the demonic religious order. They are told to wait a little longer:

> Revel. 6:10 "...wait until the number of their fellow servants and brothers who were to be killed, as they had been, was completed."

K. MARTYRED SAINTS

> Revel 7:13, "Then one of the elders asked John. "These in white robes, who are they, and where did they come from?" John answered, "Sir , you know. These are they who have come out of the great Tribulation; they have washed their robes and made them white in the blood of the Lamb. Therefore, they are before the throne of God."

> Revel 15:2, "And I saw in heaven what looked
> like a sea of glass (raptured Christians), mixed
> with fire (protected Jews on fire for the Lord).

And standing beside the sea are those who have been victorious over the beast and his image and over the number of his name. They held harps given them by God and sang the song of Moses the servant of God and the song of the Lamb."

There could be as many as tens of thousands tortured and killed during the first half of tribulation, because of their faith in Jesus the Christ. Many more will give their life to Christ as a result of the 144,000 servants of God who are sealed for their protection. They are discipling the new converts and preparing them to come to the Lord at the second harvest of believers. They have evaded the forces of evil which are out to kill them.

The first harvest is the rapture when Jesus comes for His church. The second harvest will be just before Mid-tribulation in preparation for God's two Witnesses to come to the earth to minister and to prophecy. These Two Witnesses will be God's presence on earth for the last half of Tribulation.

For three and a half years of tribulation there will be a pseudo peace. An enforced peace. Any group that sets out to protest against the beast and his government will be crushed.

In Jerusalem, temple worship and sacrifices are restored just after tribulation begins and life is good. The seven year peace treaty,(covenant) holds.

> Rev. 13:8, "All inhabitants of the earth will worship
> the beast, all whose names have not been written in the
> book of life belonging to the Lamb that was slain ..."

The beast and his false prophet will rule the world with the help of Satan, the ten kings, the army , the false religion, the police and a repressive regime.

The oppression of the saints intensifies as Satan knows his time is short on the earth.

Daniel 7:21, "As I watched the horn (beast) was waging war against the saints and defeating them."

Daniel 8:24, "He, (the beast), will become very strong, but not by his own power, but (by the power of Satan). He will cause astounding devastation and will succeed in whatever he does. He will destroy the mighty men and the Holy People. He will cause deceit to prosper and he will consider himself superior."

All seems to go well for the beast, but like everything evil, things unravel.

L. BEAST DESTROYS RELIGIOUS ORDER

Revel 17:16 "The beast and the ten horns (10 kings) you saw will hate the prostitute (the false religious order)."

Why do they hate her? Because this apostate religious order rides the beast. That is, "Babylon the great, the mother of prostitutes," becomes too rich and too powerful.

This false religious order becomes more powerful than the government and its leaders. People worship the mother of prostitutes and turn their backs on the beast and the false prophet.

Revel. 17:16, " The beast and the ten horns (kings) you saw will hate the prostitute. They will bring her to ruin and leave her naked; they will eat her flesh and burn her with fire."

Real hatred and anger. WHY?

Revel 17:17, "For God has put it into their hearts to accomplish His purpose by agreeing to give the beast the power to rule, until God's words are fulfilled."

God's purpose is to destroy this false religious order. He has a plan and it will be fulfilled. God has put it into the hearts of the beast and the false prophet to destroy this false religious order. God then tells who this woman, this harlot is:

> Revel. 17:18, "The woman you saw is the great city that rules over the kings of the earth."

This great city is Rome. The woman you saw is the harlot, the mother of prostitutes, the false religious order. She rules over the kings of the earth.

The false religious order is operated by people who are in turn controlled by Satan. They have no moral standards and conscience. Killing is second nature to them. Indulging in orgies and everything unclean and detestable, everything filthy and evil is accepted as normal.

Most of these leaders and followers of the false religious order, protest the burning of their places of beast and Satan worship and the disbanding of their religious order. They are crushed and destroyed by the army of the beast and the false prophet.

God warns people who were caught in their web:

> Revelation 18:4, "Then I (John), heard another voice In heaven say: "Come out of her (the false religious order), my people, so that you will not share in her sins, so that you will not receive any of her plagues; for her sins are piled up to heaven, and God has remembered her crimes."

It is now near the Middle of Tribulation.

M. EARTH REDEEMED BY GOD

> Rev.18:1 "After this I saw another angel coming down from heaven. He had great authority and the earth was illuminated by his splendour. With a mighty voice he shouted. "Fallen! Fallen is Babylon the great. She has become a home for demons and a haunt for every evil spirit..."

Revel 14:8, "A second angel followed, (flying in midair for all on earth to hear.) and said, "Fallen! Fallen is Babylon the Great, which made all the nations drink the maddening wine of her adulteries." Revelation 18:6. Give back to her as she has given; pay her back double for what she has done. Mix her a double portion from her own cup. Give her as much torture and grief as the glory and luxury she gave herself."

Revel 18: 9 "When the kings of the earth, who committed adultery with her and shared her luxury see the smoke of her burning they will weep and mourn over her... the merchants ...will weep and mourn." Revel. 18:19, "Woe! Woe! O great city where all who had ships on the sea became rich through her wealth. In one hour she has been brought to ruin."

Those who became rich through dealing with the religious order are ruined. The churches, mosques and temples where the false religious order operated are burned to the ground. Anyone protesting the burning and destruction of Babylon and the religious order is killed. No questions asked.

N. FIRST HALF OF TRIBULATION ENDS

CHAPTER SEVEN
MID TRIBULATION BEGINS

MID TRIBULATION comes three and a half years after Tribulation starts. A new set of events and a new set of situations and characters.

A. 144,000 TAKEN TO HEAVEN

The 144,000 servants of God, Jewish evangelists from the 12 tribes of Israel are with Jesus on Mount Zion.

> Revel. 14:1, "Then I looked, and there before me was the Lamb, standing on Mount Zion, and with Him 144,000 who had his name and His Father's name written on their foreheads.

Their tour of duty ends and they are taken to heaven at Mid Tribulation.

They are Redeemed from the earth during the second harvest of the earth.

> Revel. 14:3 , "And they sang a new song before the throne and before the four living creatures and the elders. No one could learn the song except the 144,000 who had been redeemed from the earth ... they followed the Lamb wherever He goes."

After three and a half years of hell on earth, where they were hounded and in danger of being killed, these 144,000 servants of God are now safe in the arms of Jesus. It is a great day for Jesus knowing that not one was lost. Not one was imprisoned or tortured. God's protection is more powerful than the evil forces out to destroy them.

Today, God protects His own, those who love Him and worship Him.

B. SECOND HARVEST OF BELIEVERS

Another thing that happens at Mid-Tribulation is that there will be the second harvest of saints. These are the followers of Jesus. Those who have given their life to Christ and have not been coerced by the false religious system and Satan. Because they overcame the trials and testing during the first half of tribulation, and gave their life to Christ, they are eligible to be taken from the earth.

Transported to heaven at the second harvest, to be with the redeemed Church taken from the earth at the rapture before tribulation.

These transported to heaven at the second harvest, will also be in the presence of those who were martyred for their belief in Jesus as Lord, during tribulation, and are now with Him in heaven.

> Revel 14:14, John looked and saw, "a white cloud and seated on the cloud was one like Jesus the Christ."

Only Jesus knows the hearts of men and women and the location of those who love Him. So Jesus has to do the harvesting, not an angel. To show that He is royalty and deity He has a golden crown. An angel came out of the temple and called loudly:

> Revel. 14:14, "Take your sickle and reap, because the time to reap has come, for the harvest of the earth is ripe."

Those who would NOT bow the knee to the image of the beast and worship him, because they kept the commands of God and loved the Lord Jesus and professed Him as Lord of their life, are taken up to heaven at the second harvest.

Another group that is ready for harvest are the Jews that God is protecting in the desert for 1260 days, which is three and a half years. Members of the 144,000 'servants of God' have evangelized them and they are on fire for the Lord and ready to go before the throne of God. The Bible tells us that they join the raptured Christians before the throne of God.

> Revelation 15:2, "And I saw what looked like
> a sea of glass (raptured Christians) mixed
> with fire (the Jews on fire for the Lord)

There is a joining together of the children of God into one body in heaven. This body is in union with Jesus the Christ who is the head of the body. The true believers are those known as Christians, followers of Christ Jesus.

All people on earth at this time, who have accepted the Lord, are candidates for this second harvest. With Jesus as the harvester it will happen. Daniel, the prophet of old, gives a warning from God Almighty:

> Daniel 12:1 "There will be a time of distress such as has
> not happened from the beginning of nations until then.
> But at that time, your people - everyone whose name
> is found written in the book of life will be delivered."

All who did not bow to the image of the beast and take the mark of the beast, but bowed the knee to Jesus are saved. Their name is written in the Lamb's Book of Life and they are delivered and kept from the Great Tribulation. They are also delivered from the judgments to take place. They are taken by Jesus to be before the throne of God in heaven.

C. END OF SACRIFICES IN THE TEMPLE

Daniel 9:27, predicts that in the middle of Tribulation, (middle of the seven years of Tribulation) the beast will put an end to sacrifice and offerings in the temple in Jerusalem. How does this ending of sacrifices take place? Who is responsible?

> Daniel 9:27, "In the middle of the seven (years of
> Tribulation), he (the beast) will put an end to sacrifice
> and offering. "And on a wing of the temple, he will
> set up an Abomination that causes Desolation ..."

What is this abomination that causes desolation? The Beast will set up his image, which looks like him and talks like him, in a wing of the temple in Jerusalem.

This is a terrible abomination to the Jews. The Jews are so upset they quit making sacrifices and worshipping in the temple. They will never enter the temple as long as the abomination remains in the wing of the temple.

The pseudo peace which lasted three and a half years ends. It is time for the judgements of God. These judgements are the Trumpet judgements and the Bowls of God's wrath, which are poured out on the earth during the Great Tribulation.

The GREAT TRIBULATION, the last three and a half years, kicks into gear. At a time when, if God had not intervened, the planet would destroy itself.

> Matthew 24:21, Jesus warns, "For then there will be great distress, unequalled from the beginning of the world until now -and never to be equalled again. If those days were not shortened, no one would survive, but for the sake of the elect, those days will be shortened."

As you read about these judgements, you will realize how much distress and how great in scope are these judgements. They are poured out on an unrepentant, proud and at times treacherous people. These people would rather suffer torment than repent of their evil ways and come to Jesus and be saved.

D. ORDER BREAKS DOWN

There is now no Babylon, no religious order. The False Prophet tells the beast that he is god and there is no need for any other religion. All other religious organizations are banned. Only worship of the beast and Satan are allowed.

There is a gap in the enforcement of law. The members of the apostate religion enforced the law throughout the world. They enforced the laws of the government with zeal and an iron fist. Persecuting the people and the saints relentlessly.

There is now little or no local intervention or enforcement. Only a corrupt local police force and army, often under the control of the rich land owners and millionaires. Technically, they are supposed to be under the beast's control, but he has lost control, as he is convinced he is now god and invincible.

E. SECOND SEAL IS OPENED - PEACE ENDS

Revelation 6:3, "When the Lamb opened the SECOND SEAL, I heard the second living creature say, "Come", then another horse came out, a fiery red one. Its rider was given power to take peace from the earth and to make men slay each other. To him was given a large sword."

The ten kings of the earth lose control. The rider on the red horse is given "Power to take peace from the earth."

Uprisings take place and wars break out around the world. The elected officials and the government forces are unable to quell the violence and dissension.

Before the beginning of tribulation there was a peace treaty signed. A covenant for seven years. Now, at the middle of the Tribulation, this peace treaty is broken. Why will it be broken?

Because the rider on the red horse will take peace from the earth. Not only will peace be taken from the earth, but this rider "...will make men slay each other". This rider will be given a large sword. It is not a small sword which means there will be a few people killed. It's a Large sword which means millions will be killed during this time. The last half of tribulation will see a great slaughter of men and women. Billions of men and women will die.

At first the false prophet and the beast ignore these wars and uprisings, as the beast is convinced by the false prophet that he is still in control because he is now god. The beast believes that with a word or the wave of a wand, he can regain power over the whole earth. Good sense gives way to pride and arrogance.

F. GOD'S PRESENCE ARE TWO WITNESSES

With the 144,000 servants in heaven, God proceeds to bring Two Witnesses to the earth during the Great Tribulation, as His presence on the earth. John is told that the Gentiles will trample on the holy city Jerusalem for forty-two months. These are the last three and a half years of Tribulation.

> Rev. 11:3 God says, "And I will give power to my two witnesses, and they will prophesy for 1260 days, (3 ½ years)... if anyone tries to harm them, fire comes from their mouths and devours their enemies."
> Who are these witnesses? What clues are given?

> Revel 11:6 "These men have power to shut up the sky so that it will not rain during the time they are prophesying; and they have the power to turn water into blood and to strike the earth with every kind of plague as often as they want."

Elijah, the prophet of God, shut up the skies for three and a half years in Israel at the time of King Ahab and Queen Jezebel. Moses turned water into blood and sent plagues on the Egyptians. The two witnesses will most likely be the spirits of Elijah and Moses. They will prophesy, telling of the coming Trumpet Judgements and the pouring out of the Bowls of God's wrath. As well, they will announce the opening of the seals of the scroll, which Jesus received from His Father.

Those affected by the judgements will blame the two Witnesses and hate them for what they predict. The residents on earth will have their lives compromised and will endure much pain and suffering. They will want to die rather than suffer the judgements put upon them, but death will evade them.

They suffer because they will not renounce their evil ways and unclean thoughts. They will not give their life to Christ Jesus and be saved.

CHAPTER EIGHT
JUDGEMENTS BEGIN

A. SEVEN TRUMPET JUDGEMENTS

> Revel 8:6 "Then the seven angels who had
> the seven trumpets sounded them."

These are the 1/3 judgements. Remember that each judgement is predicted by the Two Witnesses.

> Revel. 8:7 The first angel sounded his trumpet
> and there came hail and fire mixed with blood,
> and it was hurled down upon the earth. A third of
> the earth was burned up, a third of the trees were
> burned up, and all the green grass was burned up.

What a judgement! Hail, blood and fire burning up one third of the earth, the trees and the grass. 'All the green grass' includes the crops of rice, corn and wheat. What a catastrophe! What will people eat when the crops and all vegetables are burned up before harvest?

These first three trumpet judgements are against the earth, the sea and the waters.

> Revel. 8:8, "The SECOND angel sounded the trumpet
> and a third of the living creatures in the sea were
> destroyed and a third of the ships were destroyed."

> Revel 8:10, "The THIRD angel sounded and a great
> star fell from the sky a third of the waters turned
> bitter and many people died from the bitter water."

One third of the crops are destroyed. One third of the fish and ships are gone. One third of the earth's water is poisoned. Millions will die.

Crops of rice, corn and wheat are vital to the food supply. Fish are a staple in the diet of many. Fresh, clean water is crucial. Loss of one third will make a devastating impact on the earth and on mankind. Famine on a world wide scale will happen and be devastating. Contaminated water will cause many to become ill and many will die.

Some of these judgements are possibly the result of our pollution of the planet. Our passion for a high standard of living; especially for travelling in large cars and trucks, SUV's, and in planes that consume massive amounts of fuel, will put too many green house gasses into the atmosphere. The impact of such pollution might partially be responsible for some of these destructive and repressive judgements coming against the earth.

> Revel 8:12 "The FOURTH angel sounded and a third of the sun, moon and stars were struck so a third of them turned dark. A third of the day was without light and also a third of the night."

People will not be able to work in the dark. The earth will grow cold from lack of heat from the sun. People will not be able to keep warm and those with compromised immune systems will suffer relapses and many will die of pneumonia and other illnesses. With a reduction of light and heat many will become despondent and will commit suicide. They will turn on each other and become brutal and violent.

Before the next trumpet judgments are sounded by the angels, an EAGLE (type of angel), flies through midair and proclaims to the inhabitants of the earth:

> Revelation 8:13b, "Woe! Woe! Woe to the inhabitants of the earth, because of the trumpet blasts about to be sounded by the other three angels."

This Eagle, which is a type of angel, is warning the inhabitants of the earth that the following Trumpet judgements are going to become even more devastating and more deadly than the previous judgements. Why is God sending this Eagle messenger? He wants to give people a chance to come to Jesus and be saved. Bow the knee to Jesus and have their sins forgiven. A chance to change their life style and be part of the Kingdom of God. A chance to claim the protection of a loving God through these times of trials and severe testing.

Will many come to the Lord and be saved? Not likely. They are too steeped in their corrupt ways and evil deeds. However, there are converts during the Great Tribulation.

> Revel. 9:1, "The FIFTH angel sounded his trumpet and a terrible scene unfolded. A star (bright angel), came to the earth and opened the Abyss. Smoke arose from it like smoke from a giant coal burning furnace or a volcano. The sun and sky were darkened. No sunlight or moonlight. Absolute darkness.

Out of the smoke came locusts given the power of scorpions. Scorpions have a painful sting as it is laced with chemicals which are irritants. The locusts were told:

> Revel 9:4, "... do not harm the grass... or any plant or tree, but only those people who do NOT have the seal of God on their foreheads.

During the Great Tribulation, the second half of Tribulation, God will seal those who worship Him and those who love Jesus the Christ, and obey His commands. Never again will God allow the beast or Satan to make war against the saints. No more torture, killing and persecution of those who belong to God and love the Lord Jesus. The plagues will have no power over them.

These new converts are protected and sealed by a loving God during this time of great trials. These scorpion-like beings have the power to torture but not to kill. The locusts are weird looking insects.

> Revel. 9:7, "The locusts looked like horses ready for battle. On their heads they wore something like crowns of gold, and their faces resembled human faces. Their hair was like women's hair, and their teeth were like lion's teeth."

> Revel. 9:9, tells us that they wore breastplates of iron
> and the sound of their wings was like the thundering
> of many horses and chariots rushing into battle.

When people on earth hear this thundering noise they become paranoid, knowing that they will be stung by any locust that comes near to them.

> Revelation 9:10, "They had tails and stings like
> scorpions, and in their tails they had power
> to torment people for five months."

They had tails like scorpions with which to sting. Not powerful enough to kill but very painful. The pain from one sting could last for weeks or months. People are in great agony. The pain is excruciating. People want to die but death eludes them.

> Revelation 9:11, "They had as king over them
> the angel of the Abyss, in Greek, Apollyon.

The locust king is an angel of the Abyss. The Abyss is where Satan is thrown during the Millennial reign of Jesus. A place where those slated for hell thrive in their despicable and immoral ways. This king over the locusts is the destroyer, a fallen angel whose name in Hebrew is Abadon and in Greek, Apollyon. Who is also known as the avenger.

Yet many people would not give up their evil ways and worship God and Jesus the Christ. They are trapped in the web of deceit, lust, rebellion and idolatry which Satan advocates and encourages.

People on earth know that those who belong to God and Jesus are protected, yet they love their evil ways and their sins more than being protected by a loving and caring God.

The SIXTH angel sounded his trumpet and a command from heaven told them to:

> Revel. 9:14 "Release the four angels who are
> bound at the great river Euphrates. They are
> released to kill a third of mankind. The number
> of the troops was two hundred million."

These four fallen angels (controlled by demons) have been bound for many years awaiting this time when they will devastate the earth and cause calamity in the lives of many.

They are bound by God because they are slaves to Satan. At one time they were angels of God, but they have been tempted to turn away from God by Satan's lies and deceit. They are now fallen angels doing the bidding of the evil forces of darkness.

These fallen angels are loosed by the command of God to go out and kill one third of the remaining inhabitants of the earth. Some of these people killed are those who will not turn from their wicked ways and be saved by a loving Saviour. Others are innocent persons who are in the wrong place when this army passes through their towns and villages. These people are killed by fire, smoke and brimstone.

Fire from thermo-nuclear weapons, clouds of smoke and brimstone will destroy whole towns and villages as well as wreaking havoc in cities.

This army of two hundred million is formed in the east by China and other Asian countries and nations. Marching through many countries of East Asia and destroying those who oppose them and try to stop them. They are on a killing and destruction rampage. Countries who have a vendetta, will take this chance to create havoc on their enemies by deploying members of the two hundred million army from the East to kill and destroy their adversary.

All these killings bring pleasure to the four despicable angels freed from captivity at the Euphrates River. With the help of Satan, these four angels of hell orchestrate this horrific mission of mass mayhem and destruction.

> Revel. 16:12, "The Euphrates was dried up to prepare the way for the kings of the East."

These 'kings of the East,' the Asian armies, are being led by the four death angels who were bound at the river Euphrates. Bound because God knows they are dangerous and ruthless

> Revel 8:20, "The rest of mankind that were not killed by these plagues still did not repent of the works of their hands; they did not stop worshipping demons, and idols

of gold, silver, bronze stone and wood - idols that cannot see or hear or talk. Nor did they repent of their murders, their magic arts, their sexual immorality or their thefts."

It was not only the destruction carried out by the death angels and the armies that kill one third of the population of the earth. There are also plagues sent upon the inhabitants of the earth by the Two Witnesses, which kill even more inhabitants of the earth. The Bible tells us that the Witnesses could send any type of plague as often as they felt necessary.

Those who were not killed by the death angels and the plagues sent upon the land, still did not repent of the evil works of their hands. They did not stop worshipping idols. Nor did they repent of the heinous crimes they had committed. They loved their magic arts, sexual immorality, murders and thefts, more than they love the Lord Jesus Christ and God Almighty.

B. THE THIRD SEAL IS OPENED

The THIRD SEAL is opened by
the Lamb, Jesus the Christ.

Revel. 6:6, "... I heard the third living creature say, 'Come', I looked and there before me was a black horse! It's rider was holding a pair of scales in his hand. I heard a voice say, "A quart of wheat for a days wage, and do not damage the oil and the wine."

Because of the wars which are breaking out, and because the grass and crops are burned up and the one third of the sea life gone, and the plague is on fresh water, food is scarce and prices sky rocket out of control.

As a result of the wars and mayhem, truckers are not safe on the road. The market system breaks down. Food becomes a scarce commodity.

Revel 6:6, "A quart of wheat for a days wages,
and do not damage the oil and the wine."

For the poor this is a time of famine and starvation. They have to pay a days wage for enough food for one or two meals for a family of four. Food is only one item in the household budget. There is rent, electricity, water as well as medicine and other necessities. These necessities are out of reach for most as wages are low and jobs are scarce.

For the rich who have control of the food supply, the oil and the wine flows. Poor people are dying of starvation while the rich party and enjoy life. "... do not damage the oil and the wine." Commodities which are out of reach for the poor, are abundant for the rich. Food is plentiful and resources abound.

This causes the poor and suffering people to become enraged. Riots, wars and conflicts break out all over the earth. More people are killed. If you are not rich, or not employed by the rich and powerful, your chance of survival is diminished. There is little or no help from the government as it is in a state of disarray.

C. THE FOURTH SEAL IS OPENED

When the Lamb of God opened the FOURTH SEAL, there before him was a pale horse. It's rider was named Death, and Hades was following close behind.

> Revel. 6:7, "They were given power, over a
> fourth of the earth, to kill by sword, famine and
> plagues and by the wild beasts of the earth."

Revelation 6:8, tells us that they, "death and Hades", were given power over a fourth of the population of the earth to kill.

This condition comes as the result of the wars, the lack of food and the rebellions taking place on the earth. One quarter of the earth's population at that time is approximately one billion people.

This does not affect those who are sealed and protected by God Almighty.

These unrepentant people are killed by the sword which are wars, shooting and murders. People become fierce as they fight for food, clean water and the right to live a decent life without worrying about where the next meal will come from.

Armies are formed to protect the rich. These soldiers kill anyone who threatens their employer. The rich are the means of the soldier's families survival.

Hundreds of thousands die from famine as food is scarce and at times completely unavailable with the breakdown of the market system.

Crops grown by farmers and wealthy land owners are protected twenty four hours a day. If anyone is caught trying to steal a carrot or a cob of corn, they are either shot of taken as a slave and often become a member of the owner's army or bodyguard.

Plagues are sent upon the earth by the Two Witnesses of God. When the bodies resistence breaks down from lack of a balanced diet, plagues have a devastating effect on a person. Not being able to fight the bacteria from the plagues, death is often the final result.

The wild beasts of the earth are also slated to kill many. Possibly packs of wild beasts will invade settlements. As the food supplies dwindle and the animals are left with nothing, they will try to claim their share by killing livestock and even killing people in order to survive. This will be a time of survival of the fittest and the most aggressive and cunning.

Revelation 9:15, A further one third of the earth's population are killed by the invading armies from the East led by the four death angels. They kill another 1 ½ billion people. This army also causes much devastation and destruction. Complete towns and villages are destroyed beyond recognition. Cities are also attacked and sustain great damage.

One half of the earth's population is killed, when one third and one quarter of the earth's inhabitants are annihilated.

Plus all those killed in wars and those beheaded by the beast. As well as those harvested from the earth at the rapture and second and third harvest.

The population of the earth in this seven year period is decimated.

But those who have the seal of God on their foreheads are protected by God.

The two Witnesses of God are predicting each of the trumpet blasts and each of the seals that are opened by the Lamb of God. Instead of giving honour to these two Witnesses, the people on earth curse them and come against them blaming them for the punishment caused by their own evil ways and despicable actions.

If rebellious people get too close and try to harm these Two Witness, fire comes from their mouth and destroys their adversaries.

> Revel 11:3, God tells us that He will give power to His two witnesses, and they will prophecy for 1,260 days (3 ½ years). The last half of tribulation.

The Witnesses are given power to "strike the earth with every kind of plague as often as they want," and to stop the rains from falling.

D. SEVEN BOWL JUDGEMENTS

> Revel 16;1, "Then I heard a loud voice from the temple saying to the seven angels, "Go pour out the seven bowls of God's wrath on the earth."

> Revel, 16:2 The FIRST ANGEL went and poured out his bowl on the land, and ugly and painful sores broke out on the people who had the mark of the beast and worshipped his image."

Ugly and painful sores broke out on people who would not worship God Almighty and Jesus the Christ. Only on those who have the mark of the beast and have worshipped his image.

Those sealed by God are protected and are immune when it comes to seals, plagues, trumpet judgements and the bowls of God's wrath poured out on the nations.

> Revel 16:3 The SECOND ANGEL poured out its Bowl on the sea, and it turned into blood like that of a dead man, and every living thing in the sea died.

No more ships, fish, seals, whales or shell fish. Those who rely upon the sea for a living are now without a source of sea food. Many will have to rely on rice and other carbohydrates. It will mean that they will not have a balanced diet. No omega three or proteins.

> Revel. 16:4, The THIRD angel poured our his bowl on
> the rivers and springs of water, and they became blood.

Moses sent the same plague on the Egyptians.

Pharaoh decreed that all Hebrew boys born at that time were to be thrown into the Nile river, causing the river to run red with the blood of innocent babies.

Why did he give this order to the midwives? It was because the Hebrews in Egypt were multiplying at such a great rate. The Bible tells us that seventy relatives of Jacob entered Egypt at the time Joseph was second in command to Pharaoh. After four hundred and fifty years, the Hebrew's population reached nearly three million.

Pharaoh was afraid that an invading army might recruit the Hebrew men to fight against him. For that reason he ordered that boy babies to be drowned, as they would be the soldiers of the next generation and of the future.

The Angel in charge of the waters tells God that he is justified in these judgements because:

> Revel. 16:5, "...You have so judged; for they have
> shed the blood of your saints and prophets, and you
> have given them blood to drink as they deserve."

E. THE FIFTH SEAL IS OPENED

> Revel 6:9, "When the Lamb opened the FIFTH SEAL,
> I saw under the altar the souls of those who had been
> slain because of the Word of God and the testimony
> they had maintained. They called out in a loud voice ,
> "How long, Sovereign Lord, holy and true until you judge
> the inhabitants of the earth and avenge our blood."

They were given a white robe and told to wait until the killing of their fellow servants had been completed. They are the martyrs of the Tribulation who were slain because they would not deny their love of Jesus under any circumstance.

> Revel. 16:8, The FOURTH ANGEL poured out his bowl
> on the sun, and the sun was given the power to scorch
> people with fire. They were seared by the intense heat
> and they cursed the name of God, who had control over
> these plagues, but they refused to repent and glorify him.

God possibly brought the earth closer to the sun and the heat was intense. Or perhaps the ozone layer was greatly depleted by God, which caused the rays from the sun to be intensified. God is not limited. He can work supernaturally to achieve his goals. We can only surmise.

I have had painful sunburns during my life. So painful that I found it hard to wear clothes and lie down to sleep. I can imagine how painful it will be when people are seared by the intense heat of the sun.

I have also lived in the tropics and know how hot it can be. Praying for a wisp of cool air, but the air is hot and humid.

But these people refused to cry out to God and glorify him. They will not repent of their evil ways and change their sinful nature and come to Jesus and be saved.

> Revel 16:10, The FIFTH ANGEL poured out his bowl
> on the throne of the beast, and his kingdom was plunged
> into darkness. Men gnawed their tongues in agony and
> cursed the God of heaven because of their pains and their
> sores, but they refused to repent of what they had done.

Intense heat and now the earth is without the sun, 'plunged into darkness' which is going from one extreme to another. In places like the tropics, being without heat from the sun can cause great hardship as they rely on the sun to heat their homes and keep them warm; grow their crops and produce a harvest.

People, who worship the beast, are still in agony from the ugly and painful sores all over their bodies. They gnaw their tongues in agony. They are writhing in pain.

They know people who have given their life to Christ and are protected by God have no sores.

Yet these people, who 'gnaw their tongues in agony' are so addicted to their drugs, other substances, lusts and evil desires that they would rather 'writhe in pain' than go through withdrawal, give up their evil ways and come to Jesus and be protected by God Almighty.

The darkness does not affect the believers as they are praying continually and giving thanks to God in every circumstance.

> 1 Thessalonians 5:16, "Be joyful always; pray continually; give thanks in all circumstances, for this is God's will for you in Christ Jesus."

Yet the people controlled by Satan will not repent of what they have done. These people will not change their ways. They refuse to give up their evil ways and sinful desires and worship God and His son Jesus the Christ.

Daniel tells of a vision he had:

> Daniel 11:36 "The king (the beast) will do as he pleases. He will exalt and magnify himself above every god and will say unheard of things against the God of gods, (God Almighty). He will be successful until the time of wrath is completed, for what has been determined must take place."

The beast is given power at this time to do as he pleases. Except, he is not able to touch God's chosen people as they are sealed by God. God has given him free reign on the earth. He has power over the press, radio and television where he has writers and reporters tell how great he is. He exalts himself and magnifies his accomplishments, making out that he is god. He is blaspheming God Almighty and Jesus the Christ. He is telling lies, inspired by Satan, profaning the Holy ones and the saints.

He will be successful until the time of God's wrath. Then God's wrath will be unleashed against him. What has been determined to take place is revealed in the Revelation of Jesus the Christ. It will take place in God's time and in God's way.

> Daniel 11:40 "At the time of the end the king of the South will engage him (the beast and his army) in battle."

At this time in history many wars are breaking out. The beast has lost control of the regions of the earth. He is seething. He sets out to conquer the world by force.

The first time the beast and Satan conquered the world it was by deceit, coercion, and threats of nations being annihilated if they refused to be under his control. At that time there was chaos and the nations were in distress and confusion.

Now the nations are fragmented and have their own armies with which to fight back. At this time the beast and Satan have to wage war in order to take back control of the earth. The beast forms an army and starts his effort to regain the earth by controlling regions of the world by force and by crushing rebellions.

> Daniel 11:40b, "He, (the beast), will invade
> many countries and sweep through them
> like a flood. ... Egypt will not escape."

The beast starts his campaign in Europe and is successful. He then moves his army into Africa. He has a large army that is mobilized and equipped with the latest weaponry. There is little resistance. His army is superior to that of the regions being invaded. People who oppose him are slaughtered. There is no mercy.

> Daniel 11:44 "But reports from the East and the North
> will alarm him (the beast), and he will set out in great rage
> to destroy and annihilate many. He will pitch his royal
> tents between the seas and the beautiful holy mountain."

The beast is waging war in Africa. Sweeping through nations with great success. His vision of the world under his command is running smoothly.

Reports from the North and East states that troops are forming and heading towards Israel. This upsets the beast as his quest to take control of the earth has to be put on hold and he has to contend with an invasion of Israel.

The first army ready for the battle of Armageddon is now in Israel camped between the Mediterranean Sea and Mount Zion. It is the army of the beast.

> Daniel 11:40 "The king of the North will
> storm out against him with chariots and
> cavalry and a great fleet of ships."

The king of the north is Russia and its allies. They have gained knowledge that Israel is going to be invaded by an army from the East. They believe that the title deed to Israel will be awarded to the army that is victorious. They form an army and advance toward Israel with tanks, infantry as well as planes and rocketry. They also send an armada of ships armed with weaponry and fighter planes.

F. THE SIXTH SEAL IS OPENED

At this time, Jesus will open the SIXTH SEAL, Revel. 6:12, There will be a great earthquake. The sun will turn black and the moon will be blood red. Stars in the sky will fall to earth. The sky will recede like a scroll, rolling up, and every mountain and island will be removed from its place.

When an atomic bomb of great magnitude strikes, it has been reported that it is as if the sky recedes, rolling up on itself with a rushing wind, great smoke and intense heat. Massive destruction comes from such a blast. Cities and towns can suffer severe damage. Millions can be killed by the force of the blast, the heat and radio active materials.

The nuclear attacks cause a great earthquake. The mushroom clouds obliterate the sun's rays and turn the moon blood red. The nuclear attacks and the great earthquake is so powerful that mountains and islands are adversely affected. The mountains will be moved from their place, some shattering while others are rocked out of place. Large islands will tilt and shift from their moorings. Smaller islands will sink beneath the ocean.

> Revel. 6:15,16- Then the kings of the earth, the princes,
> the generals, the rich, the mighty and every slave and
> free man hid in caves and among the rocks in the
> mountains. They called out to the mountains and rocks,
> "Fall on us and hide us from the face of him who sits
> on the throne and from the wrath of the Lamb!

Who did these rich and mighty, slave and free pray to and call out to? They called out to the mountains and the rocks. These are inanimate pieces of rock and slabs of marble and shale, which have no power or no Spirit.

They were afraid to call out to God and Jesus because they are hiding from the face of him who sits on the throne. Knowing that their lives have not been lived according to the commandments of God, and that they have trespassed and are living a sinful life, with no forgiveness. They hide in the rocks and cry out to the rocks to hide them. They fear God and Jesus because they know they are candidates for the wrath of God.

> Revelation 6:17, "For the great day of their (God and Jesus) wrath has come, and who can stand?"

This will probably be an atomic attack which terrifies the rich and mighty, the slave and the free. Possibly caused by the four angels from the Abyss while leading the army of 200 million men from the East, as they travel toward Israel ready for the great battle. On their way this army kills one third of the earth's population. Plagues kill millions more. What a devastation!

The armies will travel through the countries of India, Indonesia, Vietnam, Cambodia, Japan, Korea and most East Asian countries. They are led on their killing rampage by the four demonic angels under the control of Satan. They are bent on killing and destroying everything that is created by God Almighty.

> Zephaniah 1:14, "The great day of the Lord is near-near and coming quickly. The day will be a day of wrath, a day of distress and anguish a day of trouble and ruin."

> Zechariah 14:2 "I will gather all the nations to Jerusalem to fight against it; the city will be ransacked and the women raped. ... then the Lord will go out and fight against those nations as he fights in the day of battle."

CHAPTER NINE
JESUS TAKES BACK TITLE DEED TO THE EARTH

A. JESUS TAKES BACK THE EARTH

In Revelation 10, a mighty angel comes down from heaven, robed in a cloud with a rainbow above his head; his face will shine like the sun and his legs are fiery pillars.

This is a strong angel, possibly one who has just come from the presence of God, as the angel is still shining with God's glory. The rainbow tells us that God remembers His judgement at the time of Noah and He will not judge the earth by water but rather by fire. His legs as pillars of fire, tell us that God will take back the earth by divine judgement.

With a scroll in his hand he plants his right foot on the sea and his left foot on the land. (Taking control over the land and the sea). He raises his right hand to heaven and shouts, "There will be no more delay!" The angel had John, the disciple of Jesus, eat the scroll then told him:

> Revel. 10:11, "You must prophesy again about
> many people, nations, languages and kings."

God, through Jesus the Christ, claims the title deed to the earth. The title deed which Satan wants so badly. But God had it protected in his right hand. He has given it to Jesus the Christ, the only one worthy to receive it. Jesus is now opening the seals at the appropriate times.

READ- Revelation Chapter Five.

B. JESUS REVEALS HIS OWN

Revelation 15. When the seven bowl judgements have been poured out, John the disciple of Jesus the Christ sees in heaven what looks like a sea of glass. The interpretation is the church, the raptured believers, at rest before the throne of God.

This sea is mixed with fire. These are the converted Jews who were protected by God and harvested at Mid- Tribulation. On fire for the Lord because they have given their life to Christ and are basking in His glory.

Revel 15:2, Standing beside the multitude of Christians and the messianic Jews on fire for the Lord are those believers who have been victorious over the beast.

They are all waiting to return to the earth with Jesus our Lord, when He comes to fight the battle of Armageddon and set up His thousand year kingdom on earth.

> Revel. 15: 3, "They sang the song of Moses the
> servant of God and the song of the Lamb."

C. THE TWO WITNESSES

The two Witnesses who prophesy in Jerusalem for 1260 days have been busy proclaiming what will happen during the breaking of the seals, the trumpet judgements and the bowls of God's wrath being poured out on those who will not repent of their evil ways and will not accept Jesus as their Lord and Saviour.

When what is prophesied by the Witnesses takes place, those unrepentant people on earth will become angry and curse the Witnesses. They blame them for their suffering and anguish, rather than looking inward and blaming themselves.

The Two Witnesses will testify to the people of the greatness of God Almighty and the Lord Jesus Christ. They will proclaim the gospel of God to everyone who comes within hearing distance.

Those who are swimming in sin and embracing their evil, will curse and berate the two witnesses.

> Revel 11:7 "Now when they (the Two Witnesses) have
> finished their testimony, the beast from the Abyss (Satan)
> will attack them, and overpower and kill them."

The Two Witness's bodies will lie in Jerusalem for 3 ½ days. Everyone on earth will gaze on their bodies (visually and by television) and refuse to bury them. They will gloat over their death and they will celebrate by giving gifts.

But after 3 ½ days, a breath of life from God enters the witnesses and they stand on their feet. Terror will strike those who see this miracle of God. A resurrection of the dead just like the resurrection of Jesus the Christ.

A loud voice from heaven said, "Come up here." The Witnesses go up to heaven in a cloud, while their enemies look on. At that time there will be a severe earthquake. A tenth of the city of Jerusalem collapses and 7000 people are killed.

The survivors, those who viewed the resurrection of the Witnesses of God, are terrified and give glory to God. Many are saved as a result of witnessing such a great miracle.

The SEVENTH ANGEL sounded his trumpet and there were loud voices in heaven which said:

> Revel 11:15, "The kingdom of the world has become the Kingdom of our Lord and of his Christ, and He will reign forever and forever."

D. CELEBRATION IN HEAVEN

In heaven the 24 elders, (representatives of the Church), fall on their faces and worship God. They give thanks for God's great power and the fact that He has begun to reign on earth and in the universe. They tell God it is time to reward the servants and the saints, who reverence the name of the Most High God.

> Revel. 11:19, "Then God's temple in heaven was opened, within His temple was seen the ark of the covenant. And there came flashes of lightning, rumblings, peals of thunder, an earthquake and great hailstones."

God once again displays His mighty power. He opens his temple for all in heaven to see. For the first time many see the ark of the covenant, which was on earth at the time of King David. Now it is in heaven protected by God Almighty.

On earth there is another mighty display of God's great arsenal of sights and sounds and a display of His power. Lightning and loud thunder is seen and heard throughout the earth. Another earthquake shakes the earth and is felt in many areas. Great hailstones pound the earth and cause people to run for cover.

All people on earth will know that God is alive and still in control.

> Revel 16:12, The SIXTH ANGEL poured out his bowl on the great river Euphrates and its waters dried up to prepare the way for the kings from the East.

The army of two hundred million from Asia, the kings from the east, are led by the four demonic, fallen angels. These angels please Satan with their policy of death, destruction and desolation. Helping to kill one third of the earth's population.

There are seventeen dams on the Euphrates River. As there has been no rain for years, it will not be difficult to dry up the river allowing for the crossing of this great army from the East.

CHAPTER TEN
ARMIES ARRIVE IN ISRAEL

We now have in Israel the armies from the SOUTH, (Egypt and the North African countries) as well as Sudan, Ethiopia and others.

There is the army of the WEST controlled by the beast and the false prophet, with their tents pitched between Mount Zion and the Mediterranean Sea. The army that the beast, the false prophet and Satan have mobilized to defeat all the nations of the earth in their bid to rule and have control.

The army from the NORTH has come with infantry, chariots (tanks) and ships. They are swarming over Israel, displaying their great arsenal and mighty power; flexing their muscles.

The Euphrates is being dried up to make way for the army of the kings from the EAST. Two hundred million soldiers to arrive from the countries of Asia.

This army from Asia will travel on a four lane highway constructed in the time of Mao during the cultural revolution. It is a highway through the Himalayas stretching from China through to the Middle East.

I believe it was constructed so that this army of two hundred million could come to Israel from China and the East Asian countries to fight the battle of Armageddon.

The highway stops short of the Euphrates River. No bridge was ever constructed. This army will complete whatever construction is needed to cross the river and proceed to Israel for the great battle.

A. PREPARATION FOR ARMAGEDDON

These armies will go to the Valley of Megiddo, facing each other, with Satan looking on.

B. THE SEVENTH SEAL IS OPENED

Revel. 8:1, "When Jesus opened the seventh seal, there
was silence in heaven for about half an hour." Why
is there silence in heaven for this length of time?

The most terrible time of the Great Tribulation and the most terrible atrocity the world will ever witness is about to begin. There will be so much blood shed and so many men slaughtered. God takes a time out to mourn the loss of so many humans He has created out of love and with a great purpose in mind for each one.

Revel. 16:13, "Then I saw three evil spirits that
looked like frogs; they came out of the mouth of
the dragon (Satan) Out of the mouth of the beast
and out of the mouth of the false prophet. They are
spirits of demons performing miraculous signs."

It is thought that these demons, looking like frogs, enter young men who perform miraculous signs and wonders, under the command and power of Satan.

Revel. 16:14, "... they (the frog men) go out to
the kings of the whole world, to gather them for
the battle on the great day of God Almighty...
then they gathered the kings together to the
place that in Hebrew is called Armageddon."

The demonic frog men tell the kings, and leaders of each army, that their battle is not against each other but it is against Jesus the Christ, who is coming to earth to set up His kingdom.

The frog men tell the generals and kings of the armies, "Stand united and we will defeat the Lord. The world will be ours and we can do as we please. No limits." Satan, who controls these frog men, actually believes that when they win the victory over Jesus and His army, he will rule the earth and the universe, which has been his plan and desire for eons.

Revelation 16:17-19,The SEVENTH ANGEL poured out his Bowl into the air, and out of the temple came a loud voice from the throne, saying, "It is done." Then there came flashes of lightning, peals of thunder and a severe earthquake. No earthquake like it has ever occurred since man has been on the earth, so tremendous was the quake that the great city (Jerusalem) split into three parts and the cities of the nations collapse. Every island fled (sank) and the mountains collapsed and could not be found.

> God says, "It is done." Once again He shows His mighty power with flashes of lightning, thunder and a great earthquake. Such a great quake that it split the city of Jerusalem into three parts. Not only the city of Jerusalem but cities in every nation collapse, islands sink into the ocean and seas, mountains fragment and become valleys. The greatest earthquake that has ever been recorded. What a mighty God we serve. These earthquakes become more frequent and in greater magnitude as prophesied. The armies are all in place awaiting the return of Jesus the Christ. They are ready for the battle of their lives.

CHAPTER ELEVEN
JESUS RETURNS TO THE EARTH

A. RETURN OF JESUS AND HIS SAINTS

In Heaven there is a great celebration. Jesus has made known His plan to take back the earth and to rule and reign along with the saints.

> Revel. 19:1, "After this, I heard what sounded like the roar of a great multitude in heaven shouting: Hallelujah! Salvation and glory and power belong to our God, for true and just are His judgements."

Jesus is about to win victory over the world and is about to avenge the blood of his saints. The twenty-four Elders praise God. Then the roar of a great multitude cries out:

> Revel 19: 6,7 "For our Lord God Almighty reigns. Let us rejoice and be glad and give Him glory. For the wedding of the Lamb has come, and his bride has made herself ready!"

B. WEDDING SUPPER OF THE LAMB

> Revel. 19: 9, "Then the angel said to me, "Write: 'Blessed are those who are invited to the wedding supper of the Lamb!' And he added, "These are the true words of God."

There is a wedding between Jesus the Christ and believing Christians who are in heaven, with God looking on. Blessed are those who have an invitation to the reception of the bride, the church, and the bridegroom, Jesus the Christ.

After this great event in heaven, this great celebration, John tells us that heaven was standing open. Jesus on a white horse, which means He has won the victory, is now ready to rule the earth.

> Revel.19:11, "I saw heaven standing open and there before me was a white horse, whose rider is called Faithful and True. With justice He judges and makes war. His eyes are like blazing fire, and on his head are many crowns"

"With eyes like blazing fire." Jesus sees the injustices of those who refuse to give up their evil ways and their corrupt thoughts and shameful actions. He sees those who shed the blood of the saints and His prophets. Those who have killed the Two Witnesses. It is time to avenge all the spilled blood of God's precious people.

He comes with many crowns on his head. Each crown depicts a spiritual division of His royal title and His divinity. The crowns indicate that He is supreme over everything in heaven and on earth. His robe is dipped in blood to remind everyone of the blood He shed at Calvary for the forgiveness of their sins and the healing of their bodies, minds and souls.

When the battle is over and the victory secured, Jesus will lay His crowns at the feet of God Almighty, in reverence to His Father.

> Revelation 19:12, "He has a name written on him that no one knows but himself. He is dressed in a robe dipped in blood, and his name is the word of God."

Jesus says His name is the Word of God.

> John 1:1, "In the beginning was the Word (Jesus) and the word was with God, and the Word was God.

Jesus is telling us once again that He is God and he has been with his Father since the beginning, before the universe was formed. He is God the Son, sharing divinity with His Father, God Almighty.

The armies of heaven are mounted on snow white horses.

This army consists of the raptured saints, the Jews on fire for the Lord. Also those who did not bow to the image of the beast or take the mark of the beast.

This army of God, onward Christian soldiers, are riding from heaven to the earth. They are dressed in white garments, which means that they are purified and worthy to be with the King of kings and Lord of lord.

Out of the mouth of Jesus comes a sharp sword. Ephesians 6:17 Tells us it is the sword of the Spirit, which is the Word of God. The sharp sword is the Word of God which can cut and divide. A powerful weapon with which to strike the enemy.

> Revel. 19:12-15, "His eyes are like blazing fire and on His head are many crowns. .. He is dressed in a robe dipped in blood and His name is the Word of God. The armies of heaven were following Him riding on white horses and dressed in fine linen, white and clean. Out of His mouth comes a sharp sword with which to strike down the nations."

C. BATTLE OF ARMAGEDDON

THE BATTLE TAKES PLACE

Jesus comes against the four armies numbering in the hundreds of millions. With powerful words, the sharp sword of God, and with the brilliance of his presence he defeats these armies. The battalions which come against Jesus the Christ are confused and blinded. They attack one another spilling their blood.

At the time of King Jehoshaphat of Judah, when faced by a huge army, God sent a prophet who told the king of Judah:

> 2 Chronicles 20:15, "This is what the Lord says to you: Do not be afraid or discouraged, because of this vast army, for the battle is not yours but God's... take up your positions and stand firm and see the deliverance the Lord will give you."

As God did in the past He will do again. Jesus the Christ will defeat the massive army coming against Him and His followers by trusting in God Almighty to confuse the enemy and have them destroy each other. This is the deliverance of the Lord God Almighty.

Not one member of Christ's army will have to lift a finger in battle or bear one scratch. What a mighty God we serve out of love and fear of the Lord.

D. THE THIRD HARVEST

Revel 14:17, tells of the THIRD HARVEST of the earth. This time Jesus the Son of God is not involved. The harvest does not involve Christians as they are sealed and protected by God.

Revel 14:17, Another angel came out of the temple in Heaven, and he too had a sharp sickle."

Revel. 14:18, Still another angel who had charge of the fire came from the altar and called in a loud voice, to him who has the sharp sickle; "Take your sharp sickle and gather the clusters of grapes from the earth's vine, because its grapes are ripe."

God is involved in the battle at Armageddon as He sends angels with sharp sickles to gather the harvest, which are the armies, the enemies of God's Kingdom.

Revel. 14:18b, "Take your sharp sickle and gather the clusters of grapes from the earth's vine, because its grapes are ripe."

The symbol 'cluster of grapes' represent the hundreds of millions of soldiers of the four armies at Armageddon. Two hundred million come from the East, plus the hundreds of millions who form the other three armies.

> Revel:14:19 "The angel swung his sickle on the earth, gathered its grapes and threw them into the great winepress of God's wrath."

God's wrath has come against the armies who dare to confront His Son Jesus the Christ in battle, wanting to kill Him and control the earth and the heavens.

The small and great under Satan's control want to kill Jesus the Christ, but God has a plan to give His Son Jesus the victory over the evil ones.

> Revel. 14:20 "They (the armies) were trampled in the winepress outside the city, and blood flowed out of the press, rising as high as the horses' bridles for a distance of 1600 stadia."

Blood from the slaughter of the troops is four feet deep and flowing for 200 miles down the valley of Megiddo.

> Revel 19:17, "And I (John), saw an angel standing in the sun, who cried in a loud voice to all the birds flying in midair, 'Come gather together for the great supper of the Lord, so that you may eat the flesh of kings, generals, and mighty men, of horses and their riders, and the flesh of all people, free and slave, small and great."

What a stench if the bodies of the dead soldiers and the bodies of those who were the servants and slaves of the armed forces, who also died, were allowed to decay and rot.

For this special feast God sends carnivorous birds; vultures and others to clean up the mess. He brings flocks numbering in the thousands and tens of thousands to eat the flesh of the great and the small of these invading armies.

E. BEAST AND FALSE PROPHET INTO LAKE OF FIRE

> Revel 19:20, "But the beast was captured, and with him the false prophet ... the two were thrown alive into the fiery lake of burning sulphur."

There is no trial and jury for the beast and the false prophet as these two are blatantly guilty of so many heinous crimes against humanity that the verdict is predictable and irrevocable. God has found them guilty and sentenced them to an eternity of suffering torment and pain in the fiery lake of burning sulphur.

F. SATAN INTO THE ABYSS

> Revelation 20:1, And I saw an angel coming down out of heaven, having the key to the Abyss and holding in his hand a great chain. He seized the dragon, that ancient serpent, who is the devil, or Satan, and bound him for a thousand years. He threw him into the Abyss, and locked and sealed it over him, to keep him from deceiving the nations anymore until the thousand years are ended.

These are the thousand years when Jesus will rule and reign along with the saints. Satan is locked up and cannot tempt people or deceive them. He has lost his power to lie and keep people from coming into the Kingdom of God.

> Revel. 20:12b "After that he (Satan) must be freed for a short time."

This short time comes at the end of the thousand year reign of Jesus the Christ. At this time Satan will gather an army and come against God's people.

G. JUDGES GIVEN AUTHORITY

Revel. 20:4, "I saw thrones on which were seated those who had been given authority to judge."

Who are they who will be given authority to judge?

1 Cor 6:2,3 "Do you not know that the saints will judge the world? Do you not know that the saints will judge angels?"

Do all have the authority to judge? No, this authority comes from God through the guidance of the Holy Spirit. The saints (Christians) judgement must be based on God's righteous judgement which is revealed to those who love the Lord and obey His commands.

John 5:27, "And He (God) has given Jesus the authority to judge.."

CHAPTER TWELVE
THE MILLENNIAL KINGDOM
AND REIGN OF JESUS

Those who were with Jesus in heaven are now on the earth to serve God for eternity. They will be priests and rulers in the millennial kingdom, where Jesus will rule with a sceptre of iron. Strict adherence to the law and justice. Peace will reign. The martyrs of Tribulation, having shed their blood out of love for Jesus, are rewarded. They will reign with Jesus and be in his presence for one thousand years and then for eternity.

Those who will never accept Jesus as their Lord and Saviour or bow the knee to Him, and those who do not love God Almighty and exalt Him, will be in their graves and not come to life until the thousand years have ended. Then only for a short time.

> Revel. 20:5b, "This is the first resurrection. The second death has no power over them, but they will be priests of God and of Christ and will rule with Him for a thousand years."

Jesus was the first to be resurrected from the dead. In doing so, He made a way for those who believe in Him to also avoid death. They are the ones who obey Him, keep His commands and have their anointing. They will be with Him forever and forever and be part of the First Resurrection. Christ is in union with those who love Him, his Father and the Holy Spirit.

> John 17:26, Jesus prays to His Father, "I have made you known to them, and will continue to make you known, in order that the love you have for me may be in them and that I myself may be in them."

Jesus asks His Father to let Him be in every believer for eternity so that He might walk with those who love Him, so that He can be in their lives. Christ's Spirit dwelling within all whom Jesus has made known to the Father.

Jesus is asking His Father to share the love God has for Him, with every believer so that they might feel the greatest love imaginable.

That's what it means when it says that we are in union with Jesus. His thoughts are our thoughts, his actions dictate our way of life, his life dwells within us, God's love permeates and blesses us.

We are co-heirs with Jesus the Christ, the one we love and the one who loves us.

The earth will be a much different place at the beginning of the millennium, the thousand years reign of Jesus the Christ.

A. THE WORLD IS CHANGED

The population of the world will have undergone a great reduction from the approximately seven billion inhabitants on the earth in the year Jesus came for His church at the rapture.

So many people killed just before tribulation in the war involving the enemies of the Jews. And billions more during the seven years of tribulation.

Looking back, we see that just before tribulation starts there will be an invasion of Israel by Gog, and his allies where most of a large army made up of Russians, Persians (Iraq & Iran) as well as Turkey, Germany, Northern Africa and other Arab countries, along with the Palestinian men and boys will be killed.

This army that covered the land of Israel will suffer defeat and many millions will die.

During Tribulation, at one point, one quarter of the earth's population will die from plagues, famine, the sword and wild animals.

When the army comes from the East, led by the four demonic angels of Satan, one third of the population at that time will be destroyed by atomic warfare, plagues and famine.

How many more perish during the Trumpet Judgments and the Bowl judgements is not known, but it could be millions. Hundreds of millions die at the Battle of Armageddon. Two hundred million from Asia alone.

It is mind boggling to think about such numbers of men and women dying in such a short period of time. Many of these could well be our relatives and friends, who were left behind.

As well, countries and cities on the earth will be unrecognizable because of mass devastation. The cities of the coast lands and the interior will come under attack.

Revelation 16:19, "... the cities of the nations collapse."

I often look at the beautiful city in which I live and am sad, knowing that it is possibly destined to collapse during these seven years of tribulation.

The burning of towns and cities during the cleansing of the false religious order Babylon will see millions killed. Towns and cities burned by the beast and Satan in order to get rid of their arch enemy the false religious order, the mother of prostitutes.

Isaiah 24:6b, "The earth's inhabitants
are burned up very few are left."

B. GOOD NEWS OF THE MILLENNIAL KINGDOM

The good news is that some will live through this time of Great Tribulation. I believe these will be the innocent ones who never had a chance to know about Jesus and the Kingdom of God. They are morally good people who need a chance. This chance will come when the saints return to the earth from heaven, at the coming millennial reign of Jesus the Christ.

The priests will go out to witness and minister to the inhabitants of the earth and bring lost souls into the kingdom of God.

We are told that Jesus will rule and reign with a sceptre of iron. That is, justice and peace will prevail. The laws of God will be upheld rigidly and people will be happy to live in perfect peace and in a society where love abounds.

Jesus will rule in Jerusalem and those who were with Him in heaven will be in their resurrection bodies and they will be servants of God. Doing His will during the Millennial reign and then living with God and Jesus for eternity.

When Jesus was in His resurrection body he appeared to his Disciples. The doors were locked and the windows shuttered and Jesus appeared in their midst.

> 1 Corinthians 15:42-4, So will it be with the
> resurrection of the dead. (Christians). The body
> that is sown perishable, it is raised imperishable...
> it is sown natural, it is raised a spiritual body.

Those who do not have a relationship with Jesus the Christ and God Almighty are still in their perishable bodies and will be judged.

> Jesus, in John 3:16 tells us, "...that whoever believes
> in Him, shall not perish but have eternal life."

He is telling us that if we believe that he died and rose again and profess with our lips that Jesus is Lord of our life, and bow the knee to Jesus out of love, we will not perish. Why will we not perish? It is because we will be saved by Jesus the Christ and be wrapped in the robe of righteousness.

When Jesus comes for His church, we will have our spiritual bodies which are imperishable, meaning that these resurrection bodies will allow us to go before the throne of God and they will be ours for eternity.

Bodies which are perishable will at some point perish from the presence of God. Our new bodies will be bodies just like those of Jesus the Christ.

> Romans 8:23, "...as we wait eagerly for our
> adoption as sons, the redemption of our bodies.

Christians are adopted into the family of God as sons of God, and they will be in the presence of God and of Jesus forever. They will be learning the great mysteries of the universe, which only the great teacher Jesus the Christ can teach them.

What will it be like for those in their spiritual resurrection bodies? We will appear to do the will of God wherever in the universe God sends us. Travelling in the twinkling of an eye.

> 1 Cor 15:52, "In a flash, in the twinkling of an eye." Revel 5:10 "You (Jesus) have made them (the saints) to be a kingdom and priests to serve our God, and they will reign on the earth."
>
> Revel 5:13b, "To Him who sits on the throne and to the Lamb be praise and honour and glory and power forever and forever."
>
> Revel 1:5,6, "To Him who loves us (Jesus), and has freed us from our sins by His blood, and has made us to be a kingdom and priests to serve His God and Father - to Him be glory and power forever and ever."

As well as those who endured the Tribulation and are on the earth at the beginning of the millennial kingdom, are those who have been with the Lord in heaven and are worthy to attend the wedding supper of the Lamb.

C. WHO WILL REIGN WITH JESUS?

In Revelation 15, John saw in heaven the 'church at rest'. A multitude of Christians from every corner of the earth. Those who have washed their garments in the blood of the Lamb and are sanctified (set apart for Jesus) and made holy by the sanctifying work of the Holy Spirit, by the Word of God and by the Truth of Jesus the Christ. Sealed by God for eternity.

> Ephesians 1:13, "Having believed, you were marked in Him with a seal, the promised Holy Spirit... ."
>
> John 6:27b, "On him, the believer, God the Father has placed His seal of approval."

The Saints wear the robes of righteousness and profess Jesus as Lord of their lives. Having believed in the promises of God and the love of Jesus, they are sealed for eternity. Being led on the path of righteousness by the Holy Spirit.

> Revel 15:3 "Great and marvellous are your deeds, Lord God Almighty. Just and true are your ways, King of the ages. Who will not fear you, O Lord, and bring glory to your name. For you alone are holy. All nations will come and worship before you, for your righteous acts have been revealed."

D. ALL WILL COME AND WORSHIP

Everyone on earth will come at least once a year and bow before the Lord of lords and King of kings and honour Jesus the Christ and God the Father at the temple in Jerusalem.

> Zechariah 14:16, "Then the survivors,... will go up year after year to worship the King, the Lord Almighty, and to celebrate the Feast of Tabernacles. If any of the peoples of the earth do not go up to Jerusalem to worship the King, the Lord Almighty, they will have no rain."

If people refuse to worship Jesus in Jerusalem every year, they will not be blessed.

> Isaiah 27:13b, "... and shall worship the Lord in the holy mountain of Jerusalem."

Those in their spiritual resurrection bodies will not mingle with the inhabitants of the earth. The imperishable will not have anything in common with the perishable. I believe the saints will be in Christ's presence and in the presence of God Almighty forever. Totally absorbed in His love, mercy and kindness.

E. A TIME OF PROSPERITY AND JUSTICE

These thousand years will be a time of peace and prosperity. No longer will Satan be able to deceive people and cause them to sin. People in the world will have a final opportunity to accept Jesus as

Lord of their lives and secure a place in the heavenly realm in the coming New Jerusalem.

> Amos 9:14, "I will bring back my exiled people Israel; they will rebuild the ruined cities and live in them. They will plant vineyards and drink their wine; they will make gardens and eat their fruit. I will plant Israel in their own land, never again to be uprooted."

CHAPTER THIRTEEN
A TIME OF JUDGEMENT

A. SATAN RELEASED FROM THE ABYSS

Revelation 20:7, When the thousand years are over, Satan will be released from his prison and will go out to deceive the nations in the four corners of the earth - Gog and Magog- to gather them for battle. In number they are like the sand on the sea shore.

At the end of the 1000 year reign of Jesus, Satan will be released from the Abyss and will go out to deceive all the inhabitants on earth. Those who were in their graves awaiting judgement will be released. They are alive upon the earth. All who rejected Jesus the Christ as their Savior and Redeemer and would not give up their evil ways and desires will be on the earth with Satan.

B. SATAN FORMS AN ARMY

Satan recognizes each one who he has had power over and led on the path of destruction while on the earth.

> Revel.20:9, They (Satan's army) marched across
> the breadth of the earth and surrounded the
> camp of God's people, the city God loves.

Satan forms those he has deceived and had power over on the earth into a mighty army, a great multitude, as many as the sands on the sea shore. They surround the camp of God's people in Jerusalem the city God loves.

C. GOD PROTECTS HIS OWN

God protects those who love Him and those He loves. God sends fire from heaven and devours Satan's army.

Revel. 20:9b, "But fire came down from
heaven and devoured them."

They await the final judgement.

D. SATAN INTO THE LAKE OF FIRE

Satan, who is responsible for deceiving them, is thrown into the lake of burning sulfur with the beast and the false prophet.

Revel. 20:10, "And the devil who deceived them, was
thrown into the lake of burning sulfur, where the beast
and the false prophet had been thrown. There he will
be tormented night and day forever and forever."

Once again a trial by judge and jury is not necessary. The list of Satan's atrocities over the ages has been recorded in the heavens. No chance of clemency or a hung jury. The verdict? Guilty! No questions asked.

CHAPTER FOURTEEN
GREAT WHITE THRONE JUDGEMENT

Revelation 20:11, "Then I saw a great white throne and him (Jesus), who was seated on it. Earth and sky fled from His presence and there was no place for them. And I saw the dead, great and small, standing before the throne... ."

There is no place on the earth or in the heavens for those who are being judged at this time. Earth and sky fled and there is no place for them in the universe.

The Great White Throne Judgement has Jesus seated on the throne. This judgement is for those who refused to accept Jesus as their Lord and Saviour. They have not worked out their salvation and have not had their sins forgiven. They will not confess Jesus as Lord of their lives.

Revelation 20:12 "...and the books were opened."

Notice, there is more than one book. What are these books? In order to have a fair trial the persons being judged must know why they are on trial. There are possibly three books.

First of all, Jesus the Christ will open the 'Book of the Law' often referred to in the Old Testament. Everyone is required to live according to what is written in this book.

During our time, everyone is required to live by the commandments of God Almighty as written in the Bible. These laws are also written on the hearts and minds of all who are created.

> Hebrews 8:10b, The Lord says, "I will put my laws in their minds and write them on their hearts. I will be their God and they will be my people." Deuteronomy 27:26, "Cursed is the man who does not uphold the words of the law by carrying them out."

Jesus will refer to the laws and commandments of God, which were broken by each person. Some will swear that they never heard any reference to the Law of God. God will counter with the fact that the laws were put in their mind and written on their hearts when they were born. Because of this, they know right from wrong and good from evil. God will counter with the fact that these laws of His are in their conscience and prompted them to do acts pleasing to God. But they refused to do deeds which God put in their heart.

The next book will possibly be the "Book of Works". Each person has an angel who writes down our works when on earth. Those that please God and those which are repugnant to God. As well as those done with the wrong motives. Also recorded are the times a person heard the word of God but refused to respond.
They refused to accept Jesus as Lord and be saved.

> Eccl 12:14, "For God will judge us for everything we do, including every hidden thing either good or bad."

A. CHRISTIANS ARE EXEMPT

Christians will not have to attend this Great White Throne Judgement culminating in the Second death. It is because of the grace of God, the forgiveness of sins and what Jesus did for us on the cross, that we are saved. Jesus took our confessed sins upon Himself so that we are judged and found not guilty, justified by faith through grace. Exempted from the Second death.

> Revel. 20:6, "Blessed and holy are those who have part in the first resurrection. The second death has no power over them..."

The ones who have part in the first resurrection are those who thank Jesus for going to the cross, dying and overcoming death, hell and the grave. Thanking Him for forgiving their sins and making a way back to God Almighty, and reserving a place for themselves in heaven for eternity. These are they who have given their lives to Christ and are holy and purified. Serving and praising God day and night. Sins forgiven and bound for heaven. They have already been judged and found not guilty, justified by faith and by Christ's death and resurrection.

> 1 Cor 3:13, "... his (a Christians) work will be shown for what it is, because the Day (Jesus), will bring it to light (reveal it to all). It will be revealed with fire, and the fire will test the quality of each man's work."

B. DEEDS AND WORKS JUDGED

1 Corinthians 3:11-15. If the Christian's work is built on Christ's foundation using gold, silver and costly gems, they will be revealed to all in heaven. They will then be purified by fire.

If a man's work is built on wood, hay or straw, they will be revealed to all and then they will be judged by fire and burned up.

> Revelation 3:13, "It (the Christian's work) will be revealed with fire, and the fire will test the quality of each man's work."

If a person's work survives, he or she will receive a reward. If their work is burned up that person will suffer loss (of respect). He (or she), being a Christian, will be saved but only as one escaping the flames. White garments covered with black ashes and the smell of smoke for eternity, for all in the Kingdom of God and the universe to see and smell.

C. THE LAMB'S BOOK OF LIFE

The last book is the 'Book of Life' and 'The Lamb's Book of Life.' The Book of Life has contained the name of every person born on planet earth. However, if a person has never accepted the love of Jesus, and the fellowship of the Holy Spirit, their name will be blotted out of the Book of Life.

If, during the Tribulation, a person accepts the mark of the beast and bows to his image his name will be blotted out of the book of life.

When a person lives a self-centred life never taking an active role in the church, the body of Christ; never bowing the knee to Jesus, and not having their sins forgiven, their name will be blotted out of the Book of Life.

Or for whatever reason God determines is justified, their name will be blotted out of the book of Life.

The Lamb's Book of Life contains the names of all who have given their life to Christ and are in fellowship and in union with Jesus the Christ. They have already been judged and been found not guilty, as their sins are forgiven and they belong to Jesus the Christ, who bought them with His precious blood shed on the cross. They will be with Jesus and God for eternity.

> Revel. 5:9b, "... and with your blood you purchased men for God from every tribe and language and people and nation."

> John 17:21, Jesus prays to His Father, "... Father, just as you are in me and I am in you. May they also be in us ..."

Jesus prays that all believers will be part of the trinity, part of the family of God Almighty, in union with Jesus the Christ forever.

John 17:24 Jesus prays, "Father, I want those you have given me to be with me where I am and to see my glory."

Matthew 16:27, "For the Son of Man (Jesus) is going to come with His Father's glory with His angels, and then He will reward each person according to what he has done."

Jesus tells us through these prayers, that He wants all who believe in Him and all who love Him to be with Him wherever He is in heaven and on earth; everywhere in the universe. He especially wants everyone to see His glory. Not only to see His glory but to be part of that glory.

Romans 9:23, "What if he (Jesus) did this to make the riches of His glory known to the objects of His mercy (Christians), whom He prepared in advance for glory..."

Romans 2:7, "... a wisdom that has been hidden and that God destined for our glory before time began."

Christians, who love and adore Jesus the Christ, will see the glory of the risen Lord. Jesus desires that we see his full glory and the riches of His glory. He wants to make this glory known to all who love Him and worship Him. Jesus tells us that He has prepared us for glory in the coming Kingdom. God has destined us for glory before time began. God knew us before time began and He knows our every thought and action at this very moment.

Jesus is going to come with His Father's glory, and He will reward everyone according to what he has done for the Kingdom of God and for God's glory.

THE FINAL JUDGEMENT

D. GUILTY INTO THE LAKE OF FIRE

Revel 20:13, "The sea gave up the dead that were in it, and death and Hades gave up the dead that were in them, and each person was judged according to what he had done."

The seas (the nations), gave up all those in the grave, and death and Hades gave up those waiting in hell for the final results of the judgments of God.

Revel. 20:14 "The lake of fire is the second death. If anyone's name was not found written in the book of life, he will be thrown into the lake of fire."

Matt 25:41, the King will reply, "... depart from me, you who are cursed, into the eternal fire prepared for the devil and his angels."

Finally, all who will never accept Jesus as Lord, but who follow their own evil desires will be judged and punished according to their deeds.

CHAPTER FIFTEEN
THE KINGDOM OF GOD

The Millennial Kingdom gives way to the Kingdom of God. Revel, 21:1, Then I saw a New Heaven and a New Earth, for the first heaven and the first earth had passed away, and there was no longer any sea."

The garden of Eden was beautiful beyond description. I believe God, at the time of the New Heaven and New Earth, is creating a garden on the new earth that will surpass the beauty of the garden of Eden.

> Genesis 2:1, "Thus the heavens and the earth
> were completed in all their vast array."

> 2 Peter 3:13, "But in keeping with His promise,
> we are looking forward to a new heaven and a
> new earth, the home of Righteousness."

God has prepared a place for the righteous, who are now married to Jesus in a perfect relationship, a union that will last for eternity.

A. THE NEW JERUSALEM

> Revel 21:2, "I saw the Holy City, the New Jerusalem,
> coming down out of heaven from God, prepared
> as a Bride, beautifully dressed for her husband."

The earth has been cleansed by God and those who will be with the Lord forever and forever are in this New Jerusalem. "Prepared as a Bride."

The Bride is the church, the true believers, not just one person.

Dressed in white linen, which are the righteous acts of the saints. Christians beautifully dressed in saintly robes, fit to be in the presence of Jesus the Christ.

This tells of the loving relationship the true believers have with Jesus the Christ for eternity. What a beautiful picture of heaven on earth in a place God has gorgeously prepared for those who love Him.

From the throne of God in the New Jerusalem came a loud shout:

> Revel 21:3b, "Now the dwelling of God is with men, and He will live with them. They will be His people and God Himself will be with them and be their God."

We have been allowed to be in the presence of God in our mountain top experiences. Now, we will dwell with Him forever and live our lives in His presence, in the glorious New Jerusalem.

Who is it who will live with God for eternity? Those who will be His people. Everyone must make the decision to be in God's family. They must have a desire to be sanctified and purified, leading holy and godly lives on earth in order to qualify to be in the New Heaven and New Earth.

> Revelation 21:5, He that is seated on the throne said, "I am making everything new!" then He said, "Write this down, for these words are trustworthy and true."

God tells us, "I am making everything new. For the old order of things has passed away".

> Revelation 21:4, "He will wipe every tear from their eyes. There will be no more death or mourning or crying or pain, for the old order of things has passed away."

> Revelation 21:6,7, The apostle John writes, "He (Jesus) said to me, "It is done. I am the Alpha and the Omega, the Beginning and the End. To him who is thirsty, (for righteousness), I will give to drink without cost from the spring of the water of life. He who overcomes will inherit all of this, and I will be his God and he will be my son."

All the blessings from God and Jesus are for those who overcome the world and the fleeting pleasures of the world. The blessings are for those who are in union with Jesus the Christ, and who honour and exalt God the Father. They are for those who are worthy to be in the kingdom of God.

What does this new Jerusalem look like?

> Revel 21:11, "It shone with the glory of God, and its brilliance was like that of a very precious jewel." (like a diamond with many facets)

> Revelation 21:21, "The great street of the city was of pure gold, like transparent glass."

> Revel.21:12, "It had a great high wall with 12 gates and with 12 angels at the gates. On the gates were written the names of the twelve tribes of Israel."

> Revel.21:14, "The wall of the city had twelve foundations, and on them were the names of the twelve apostles of the Lamb."

This New Jerusalem shines with the glory of God. It is magnificent and gorgeous in appearance. Gems shining in all their brilliance. It is dazzling and pleasing to the eye.

> Revel. 21:19, "The foundations of the city walls were decorated with every kind of precious stone."

You would do well to read Revelation, Chapters 21 and 22.

> Revel 21:22, "I did not see a temple in the city, because the Lord God Almighty and the Lamb (Jesus the Christ) are its temple... God gives it light and the Lamb is its lamp."

Everyone on earth and in heaven, who honours God Almighty, will walk in the light of the Lord and in the knowledge and wisdom which they will receive from God Almighty.

You thought you knew a great deal about the Kingdom of God, but the Lord will be teaching you new things throughout eternity. His wisdom is profound and He desires to share it with all in His kingdom.

> Isaiah 55:8, 9 God says "For my thoughts are not your thoughts, neither are your ways my ways, as the heavens are higher than the earth, so are my ways higher than your ways."

The saints will be in their resurrection bodies doing the will of God serving him as priests and rulers or in whatever capacity God ordains. Walking in His light and learning the thoughts of God, and the higher ways which lead from glory to glory.

B. NOTHING IMPURE WILL ENTER

> Revelation 21:27, "Nothing impure will ever enter it, (the New Jerusalem), nor will anyone who does what is shameful or deceitful, but only those whose names are written in the Lamb's book of life."

> Revel 22:12, "Blessed are those who wash their robes, that they may have the right to the tree of life and may go through the gates into the city."

> Revel. 22:13, "Outside are the dogs, those who practice magic arts, (the occult), the sexually immoral, the murderers, the idolaters, and all liars."

No one wants to be outside with such people. All people in their right mind will desire to be inside where the light of God and Jesus is the brightest, where their love is the strongest and peace flows like a mighty river.

C. THE HOLY SPIRIT WILL FLOW

> Revel 22:1 Then the angel showed me the river
> of the water of life, as clear as crystal, flowing
> from the throne of God and of the Lamb
> down the middle of the street of the city.

I believe this is the Holy Spirit which flows from the throne of God still guiding, teaching, comforting, counselling and bringing us into an even closer relationship with God Almighty and Jesus the Christ. It says that this river flows from the throne of God and of the Lamb. That only leaves the Holy Spirit to flow from the throne. Showing us that we too must flow in a more loving and caring relationship with our brothers and sisters in Christ, and with others in the universe.

Jesus was the life giving water when on earth, and He is still the life giver in the New Heaven and the New Earth.

> Revel. 22:2b "And the leaves of the trees
> are for the healing of the nations."

The healing power of Jesus and God is in the leaves of the trees and is for the healing of the nations. All are healed by these leaves in the New Jerusalem. Nations have just come through a terrible time in history. They need the healing touch of the divine healer.

> Revelation 22:3, "No longer will there be any curse."

When Adam ate of the tree which was forbidden by God, a curse came upon the whole world. One curse is that men and women are born with a sinful nature. Through this curse, people are tempted to sin again and again, and those who do not have Jesus as their Saviour, must bear these sins throughout their lifetime.

We know that only Jesus can forgive sins and remove the curse.

Jesus, when on the cross, took that curse and nailed it to the cross. But men, in their depravity, have taken it down and are still under the curse and their sins are not forgiven.

The exception are those who are born again and are in union with Jesus the Christ. They have had their sins forgiven and are saved by the grace of God. The curse has been removed from Christians and has been nailed back on the cross where it belongs.

In the New Heaven and the New Earth, the curse is cancelled as the curse came by Satan. Satan is now a non entity. There is no curse on those in the New Jerusalem.

> Revelation 22:4 "They (the believers) will see his face and His name will be on their foreheads."

Kindness, goodness, peace and joy will flow like a mighty river. All will serve God and Jesus and will see them face to face.

For many years I have longed to see the face of the Lord. Now this wish will be fulfilled.

The greatest thing for those who overcome is that God's name will be sealed on their foreheads. As sealed Christians go throughout heaven, the New Jerusalem and the universe; every heavenly being and all heavenly and universal hosts will know that we are the ones who were on earth and overcame the worldly ways.

They will know that we are the ones in union with our Lord Jesus and are blessed by God. His name on our foreheads for all in the universe to see and marvel at the grace and love of God. Jesus then gives us a warning for our time:

D. JESUS SAYS COME

> Revel. 22:7, "Behold I am coming soon. Blessed is he who keeps the words of the prophecy in this book."

Every word in the Book of Revelation, and in the Bible, has great significance and relevance. We are to keep the words in our hearts and obey what has been given us from God Almighty.

God gave us prophecy so that we can make appropriate decisions. When we do so, God is blessed and we are blessed.

Jesus says, "Behold I am coming soon..." We must not procrastinate and put off doing the will of God for us at this time. Jesus wants us to be ready when He comes.

But anyone who adds anything to the words of the book or takes away anything to change the meaning of this book of prophecy, God will add the plagues described in the book to him. God will also take away his share of the tree of life. Jesus tells us:

> Revel 22:12, "Behold I am coming soon!
> My reward is with me, and I will give to
> everyone according to what he has done."

> Revel 22:16, "I, Jesus, have sent my angel to give you this testimony for the churches . I am the Root of the Offspring of David, and the bright Morning Star."

CHAPTER SIXTEEN
ENCOURAGEMENT AND CONCLUSION

As we wait for these glorious things to happen, we know that we are still in bodies of clay. We have so much to look forward to, but we must first of all overcome the world in which we live.

We must make a decision for Christ to live in us and empower us as we live out our days on earth.

> Jesus says, Acts 1:8, "You will receive power when the Holy Spirit comes on you ... ."

> Ephesians 3:20, "Now to Him (Jesus), who is able to do immeasurably more than all we ask or imagine, according to his power that is at work within us ... ."

As we come to Jesus and are in union with Him, he tells us that we will receive power when the Holy Spirit comes upon us and dwells within us. As we pray and praise the holy name of Jesus and God Almighty, an explosion of His power and might will come from heaven and empower us to do His will.

When this power hits us, we will be able to do miraculous works; and signs and wonders will follow us, giving glory to God in heaven. As we become vessels for the power of God, He will work miraculously and supernaturally in our lives according to His will and for His purpose.

As we sing praises to the Lord, we will have days filled with love for our Saviour. Days to reach out to others in order to have them share God's love in the Kingdom of God.

We are told that God inhabits our prayers and our praises. As we pray to our Lord and praise Him in word and in song, it gives Him permission to work good in our life. God will inhabit our mind, body and soul, doing his miraculous works that we might have the fulness of his promises and his blessings.

But there are those who will not pray and praise the Lord. We are warned about what will happen to them.

In these last days on earth, Paul tells us there will be terrible times for those who will not worship God and who will not praise the name of Jesus and follow the leading of the Holy Spirit. Jesus tell us that they will be like those at the time of Noah.

> Genesis 6:12, "Now the earth was corrupt in God's sight and was full of violence. God saw how corrupt the earth had become, for all the people on the earth had corrupted their ways."

We see and read about this violence in the world today. Many people are corrupt in the sight of God and in the sight of humanity.

In the days of Noah, 'all the people on the earth had corrupted their ways.' Today it is not only violence but corruption in the corporate world and in every walk of life. People are caught stealing, lying, cheating and every form of sinful act. Terrible times with wars and atrocities. Unimaginable vice and corrupt acts which are often legitimised by many governments. Hopefully, there are those who have not corrupted their ways.

In God's sight those who do not have their sins forgiven are living in darkness. Why? Because God cannot look upon sin as sin comes through Satan.

> Ephesians 5:8, speaking to Christians, "For you were once darkness, but now you are the light of the world.

Christians are the light of the world as they have had their sins forgiven and they pray continually and praise God from a heart filled with love, peace and joy.

People who do not thank Jesus for what He did on the cross are, in God's sight, unthankful and proud. People who do not pray and praise the Lord and have their sins forgiven are seen by God as darkness. Dark beings wandering aimlessly on the earth.

Jesus goes on to tell us that there will be times of temptation, trials and testing in the lives of all on earth. When we choose not to give in to temptation and when we pass the tests, God will lift us up to be in the arms of Jesus and we will be overcomers, worthy to be in the Kingdom of God.

James, the brother of Jesus, tell us that if we persevere under these trials we will be rewarded. What is this reward?

> James 1:12, "Blessed is the man who perseveres under trial, because when he has stood the test, he will receive the crown of life that God has promised to those who love him."

We should be aware that we must not only persevere under trial, but we must pass the test, which God has given us in order to build our spiritual character. James tells us it is only promised to those who love Jesus the Christ and God Almighty.

> Revelation 19:12 tells us, "... on his (Jesus) head are many crowns."

We too, as Christians, are promised many crowns as we wait on the Lord and as we live a life pleasing to God Almighty.

> 2 Timothy 4:8, Paul tells us, "Now there is in store for me the crown of righteousness, which the Lord, the righteous judge, will award me on that day – and not only me, but also all who have longed for his appearing."

Are you eagerly awaiting the return of Jesus the Christ who will take the true believers to be before the throne of God in heaven?

Are you waiting for an angel to guide you to Jesus so that He can take you with Him in the clouds and then into heaven before the throne of God? If the answer is yes, then you will receive the crown of righteousness. Hallelujah!

> Jesus tells us in Revelation 3:10, "I am coming soon. Hold on to what you have, so that no one will take your crown."

There is also the shepherd's crown for those who bring their sheep, their flock, their congregation into the Kingdom of God.

> 1 Peter 5:4, "Be shepherds of God's flock that is
> under your care ... eager to serve ... being examples.
> And when the Chief Shepherd appears, you will
> receive the crown of glory that will never fade.

Look in the Bible and you will find other crowns that you can have when you go into heaven. We will lay our crowns at the feet of Jesus, just as He laid His crowns at the feet of His Father.

Having read this book, you have the facts that are necessary to make a decision to follow Jesus every step of the way. The way which leads into the Kingdom of God forever and forever.

Greater things are to come. As you read the book again, study it, meditate on it and teach it to others.

Read the Book of Revelation with this book as your guide. Jesus tells us in the first chapter of the book of Revelation:

> Revel 1:3, "Blessed is the one who reads the words of
> this prophecy, and blessed are those who hear and take
> to heart what is written in it, because the time is near."

I know that I desire to be blessed every day and all day. As you read the scriptures in this book, you are being blessed, when you take to heart all that is written.

My mother blessed me as I was growing up. Every day before I left for school or later for work, she blessed me. Along with the blessing came words of encouragement. "You can do anything God directs you to do." These words have kept me in the ministry doing whatever God puts in my path to do for His glory.

A. OPEN YOUR HEART TO JESUS

Jesus is knocking at the door of your heart. You must open your heart to Jesus and let Him come in. By the working of the Holy Spirit, your heart will be filled with the love of Jesus the Christ and God our Father. Once your heart is filled, you will be able to spread that love around to all you know and to all you meet.

> King David says in Psalm 119:10, "I seek
> you (Lord) with all my heart."

> 1 Peter 1:22, "... love one another from the heart."

When we seek the Lord and keep His commands and obey God out of love, we are doing what pleases God and we will find favour in His sight.

> John 14:21, Jesus says, "Whoever has my commands
> and obeys them, he is the one who loves me. He
> who loves me will be loved by my Father, and I
> too will love him and reveal myself to him."

Many people know the commands as written in the Bible, but they do not obey them. They do not respond to God's calling and will for their lives. By doing so, they miss out on the love which is poured out on those believers who have a loving relationship with God the Father and God the Son.

Everyone God created is created for a purpose. God has a purpose for our lives. When we fulfill this purpose and plan, God is blessed and we are blessed.

> Jeremiah 29:11 God says, "For I know the plans I
> have for you." declares the Lord, "plans to prosper
> you not to harm you, plans to give you hope and a
> future. Then you will call upon me and come and
> pray to me and I will listen to you. You will seek me
> and find me, when you seek me with all your heart.
> I will be found by you," declares the Lord ... .

God is in the business of prospering those who love Him. Not necessarily making them rich in the eyes of society, but making them worth something to the Kingdom of God. He wants to give us hope now and for the future. But God desires that we ask for what we need at this time in our lives. He promises that He will listen to our prayers and answer those prayers, which will be for our benefit and will bring glory to God.

You are a person, a human being, created by God and for God. You were not created as the result of a big bang in the universe. God created you for himself. It is not what do 'I' want to do with my life, but rather it is, what does God want to do with my life? It's not wondering about my goals, ambitions and dreams. It's about coming to Jesus the Christ and asking Him to send down the Holy Spirit to guide, teach, counsel, convict and control you. Leading you in love on the path of righteousness. Opening the doors of opportunity in order that you can prosper and fulfill your dreams.

We are dealing with the Creators of the universe! Not someone in an ivory tower or someone in authority, like your boss. We are loved by the greatest and most profound Beings whoever existed and whoever will exist, Jesus the Christ and God Almighty.

God and Jesus are asking us humans to come into their kingdom and be part of their family. Who in their right mind could say no to such an invitation.

Jesus prays to His Father for all believers:

> John 17:21, "... Father, just as you are in me and I am in you. May they (Christians) also be in us... "

Jesus is asking God the Father to allow His followers to be in the circle of the Trinity, which presently includes: God the Father, God the Son and God the Holy Spirit. He is asking His Father to have us share his attributes which are: His sovereignty, holiness, immutability and His omnipotence. What a lofty calling for human beings to attain to.

Jesus wants many brothers and sisters in His Father's family. He is the only son, which can be lonely. Jesus also asks His Father in heaven:

> John 117:26b, "... in order that the love you have for me be in them (The believers) and that I myself will be in them."

Jesus desires to be in union with those who love Him and His Father. He wants the same love God has for Him to flow out to all who love Him and keep His commands.

The question is, "will you accept these invitations?" If yes, then you must prepare yourself for a life with Jesus and His Father in the New Jerusalem?

B. BEING OF SERVICE TO GOD

As you read this book you will realize that you are shaped by God. Blessed with special areas of expertise and talents with which to serve God Almighty. We are each uniquely designed to do ministry. Before you were created, God had decided what he wanted you to do on the earth.

We must prepare ourselves through service to Him, to reach for the higher calling in our life. God desires that we serve him by striving to live up to our potential in whatever calling we have.

> Ephesians 2:10, "For we are God's workmanship, created in Christ Jesus to do good works, which God has prepared in advance for us to do."

C. BLESSED BY GOD

Then we will be blessed.

> Ephesians 1:3, "Praise be to the God and Father of our Lord Jesus Christ, who has blessed us in the Heavenly realms with every spiritual blessing in Christ."

It goes on to tell us about these blessings:

#1. Jesus chose us in Him before the creation of the world. Eph. 1:4
#2. He chose us to be holy and blameless in His sight. Eph. 1:4
#3. He predestined us to be adopted as His sons (and daughters). Eph. 1:5
#4. In Him we have redemption through His shed blood, the forgiveness of sins ... . Eph. 1:7
#5. The grace of God lavished on us with all wisdom and understanding. 1: 7,8

#6. We, who are the first to hope in Christ, might be the praise of His glory. 1:12

#7. Having believed, you were marked in Him with a seal, the Holy Spirit. 1:13

#8. The Holy Spirit, a deposit guaranteeing our inheritance until redemption. 1:14

As we understand and fulfill God's purpose for our life, we are guaranteed so many blessings that we will not be able to contain them.

Greater Things Are to Come for those who love the Lord and serve God Almighty.

D. SHARE WHAT YOU KNOW

As you study this book, make it a point to share it with others. Help your family, your relatives, your friends and colleagues have the opportunity to become enlightened and make a decision to avoid the Tribulation by trusting in the Lord, who will keep them from the coming wrath. It will save their life and their soul.

> Daniel 12:3, "Those who are wise will shine like the brightness of the heavens, and those who lead many to righteousness like the stars forever and forever"

Who are the wise ones whose light will shine? They are the followers of Jesus the Christ. Imagine shining like the brightness of the heavens for eternity.

Jesus took three of His disciples up a high mountain.

> Matthew 17:1, "... Jesus took with Him Peter, James and John, the brother of James, and led them up a high mountain by themselves. There He was transfigured before them. His face shone like the sun, and his clothes became white as the light."

Jesus is showing the disciples what he will be like in heaven, when His glory is returned to Him. It is also a small foretaste of the glory the disciples and Christians will receive when they are transported into heaven.

Imagine a person whose face shone like the sun when on the earth. His glory will shine even brighter when he is in heaven. Not only did Jesus shine brightly but his clothes became white as the light.

This is what the wise ones of Daniel 12:3 will be like. Those who have given their life to Christ will shine like the brightness of heavens. And those who lead many to righteousness will shine like the stars forever and forever.

What a great promise to those who love the Lord and are in union with Jesus the Christ.

One ministry you can do is to form a Bible Study Group and use this book as your study guide. I know that I will be using this book as a study guide, when I teach in the College.

You can give a copy of the book as a gift of life to those you love and to those who need the Lord in their life.

If you are searching for a church, the body of Christ, pray that the Holy Spirit will guide you as you make the decision to be in that particular spiritual family. Discern the spirit that guides the believers. If it fits with your spirit, then you will have the opportunity to worship, minister and be part of the body. You will make a difference as you use your God given talents to edify and build up the body of Christ. As you practice your spiritual gifts, the church will be blessed, God will be blessed and you too will be blessed.

If, for some reason, you are not being filled and not growing in your faith and in your spiritual walk, pray about it and perhaps consider a move to another more compatible and spirit filled church.

Realize that we are all being perfected. No one is perfect except for our Lord and Saviour Jesus the Christ. So don't expect to find that perfect fellowship, that perfect body of Christ, that perfect minister or pastor. Many times, it only takes one like you to motivate others and activate others in order to build up the body of Christ.

<u>Use this book</u> as a tool to give others the necessary knowledge to have a closer walk with Jesus.

Revelation 22:17, The Spirit and the bride say,
"Come!" And let him who hears say

"Come!"
Whoever is thirsty, let him come; and whoever wishes, let him take the free gift of the water of Life.

Jesus and the church, his bride, are asking people to come and be filled with life giving water, which is the word of God and the transforming power of Jesus the Christ.

Only Jesus the Christ can forgive your sins. Only Jesus the Christ can save your soul. Only Jesus the Christ can get you into heaven.

It's all Free. It's the free gift of God for those who will ask. God will never force anyone to take what they will not use.

All you need to do is daily ask Jesus to "Come!" Come into your life and fill you with His Spirit. Reveal His plan for you to reach out and bring others into the Kingdom.

Call out and ask Jesus, " Come Lord Jesus, come and fill me, guide me and use me for your glory."

Jesus is waiting for you to knock, to seek and to ask for eternal life in the New Heaven and the New Earth. It is yours for the asking.

God bless you and yours.